It's My State!

MISSOURI

The Show-Me State

Doug Sanders and Gerry Boehme

Cavendish Square

New York

Published in 2016 by Cavendish Square Publishing, LLC
243 5th Avenue, Suite 136, New York, NY 10016

Library of Congress Cataloging-in-Publication Data

Sanders, Doug, 1972-
Missouri / Doug Sanders and Gerry Boehme.
pages cm. — (It's my state!)
Includes bibliographical references and index.
ISBN 978-1-6271-3244-2 (hardcover) ISBN 978-1-6271-3246-6 (ebook)
1. Missouri—Juvenile literature. I. Boehme, Gerry. II. Title.
F466.3.S255 2015
977.8—dc23

2015022182

Editorial Director: David McNamara
Editor: Fletcher Doyle
Copy Editor: Rebecca Rohan
Art Director: Jeffrey Talbot
Designer: Alan Sliwinski
Senior Production Manager: Jennifer Ryder-Talbot
Production Editor: Renni Johnson
Photo Research: J8 Media

Printed in the United States of America

MISSOURI
CONTENTS

A Quick Look at Missouri 4

1. The Show-Me State 7
Missouri County Map 10
Missouri Population by County 11
10 Key Sites 14
10 Key Plants and Animals 20

2. From the Beginning 23
The Native People 26
Making Walnut Shell Turtles 30
10 Key Cities 34
10 Key Dates in State History 43

3. The People 45
10 Key People 48
10 Key Events 54

4. How the Government Works 57
Political Figures from Missouri 62
You Can Make a Difference 63

5. Making a Living 65
10 Key Industries 68
Recipe for Black Walnut Cake 70

Missouri State Map 74
Missouri Map Skills 75
State Flag, Seal, and Song 76
Glossary 77
More About Missouri 78
Index 79

State Bird: Bluebird

This delicate songbird is known for its striking blue feathers. A bluebird usually reaches about 6 to 7 inches (15 to 17.8 centimeters) in length. When the bluebird population started to shrink, concerned Missourians put up thousands of nesting boxes to help the species thrive.

State Fossil: Crinoid

Fossilized crinoids are the remains of animals that lived millions of years ago in the vast sea that once covered the state. Nicknamed "sea lily" because they sometimes resemble a plant, these ancient crinoids are related to today's starfish and sand dollar. About six hundred species of crinoid live in oceans today.

State Mineral: Galena

Galena is a major source of lead ore. Galena is dark gray and breaks into small cubes. It was adopted as the state's mineral in 1967 to acknowledge Missouri as the top lead producer in the United States. Lead is used to make batteries, electronics, and protective coatings.

MISSOURI

State Musical Instrument: Fiddle

Fur traders first brought the fiddle to Missouri in the late 1700s. Playing music was a main source of entertainment, and a fiddle player was highly respected for his or her talents. The instrument, which helped shape the state's rich musical heritage, was officially adopted in 1987.

State Reptile: Three-Toed Box Turtle

In 2007, the three-toed box turtle was declared the state reptile. These animals are native to the south-central United States and are often kept as pets. Shy and quiet, they are small, gentle and don't bite. They get their name from the three toes on their back feet.

State Tree: Flowering Dogwood

This elegant tree can grow more than 30 feet (9.1 meters) tall. It was adopted as the state tree in 1955. The tree grows in clusters across the state, but is most often found in the Ozarks and in several counties north of the Missouri River.

Rich soil makes much of Missouri ideal for farming and provides perfect growing conditions for grass that can feed grazing cattle.

The Show-Me State

The state of Missouri literally sits at the crossroads. It is where the western prairie meets the eastern woodlands and where the Northern Plains join the lowlands of the Southeast. It is also where two of the nation's mightiest rivers, the Missouri and the Mississippi, join forces. Numerous settlers once rolled across this land, earning the city of St. Louis (or Saint Louis) the nickname "Gateway to the West." Many people passed through this gateway and continued west, while others stayed to build lives in the heartland. Missourians only have to look around them to see the gifts their state has to offer. Rushing streams, lush forests, and glistening lakes are just some of the reasons millions of visitors arrive each year, declaring, "Show me Missouri."

The Big Muddy

While it is true that the great Mississippi River unrolls along Missouri's eastern border, the state's most important waterway is the Missouri River. The source of the Missouri River lies far to the west, in the state of Montana. There it flows strong and clear. By the time the river reaches Missouri, however, its color has usually changed. Murky and dark, the river picks up dirt and silt as it winds its way to the Mississippi. For this reason, the Missouri has earned the nickname "the Big Muddy."

The Missouri River flows 2,341 miles (3,767 kilometers) from Montana until it joins the Mississippi River.

The Big Muddy acts as a natural dividing point. It creates a rough border between northern and southern Missouri, splitting the state in two, with the bottom section being the somewhat larger part. The Big Muddy also helps to divide the state's landscape. Though dense forests, low hills, and vast grasslands are found across the state, each section of Missouri has its own sense of beauty.

The Northern Plains

The Northern Plains are also called the central lowlands. These lowlands include the parts of Missouri north of the Missouri River, as well as parts of Iowa, Nebraska, and Kansas. Hundreds of thousands of years ago, the Northern Plains of Missouri were covered by glaciers. As the massive chunks of ice eventually headed north, they left behind soil rich in nutrients and mineral deposits. Today, the fertile soil of northern Missouri makes the area ideal for farming. Corn and soybeans thrive among the rolling grasslands while cattle graze in the fields.

Missouri Borders	
North:	Iowa
South:	Arkansas
East:	Illinois Kentucky Tennessee
West:	Kansas Nebraska Oklahoma

Because of all this Ice-Age action, the northern part of the state is also called the Dissected Till Plains. That is because the glaciers tilled, or ground and mashed up, tiny pieces of rock and soil. Once the glaciers left the region, rivers and streams dissected, or cut through, the smooth surface of the till plains. Today, the Northern Plains stand as a series of river valleys bordered by higher, hill country. In some sections, though, the land levels off to become almost perfectly flat. These areas still bear traces of the original till plain. The flattest part of the Northern Plains can be found in a narrow strip just west of the Mississippi River. There, the surface of the land was not broken up by water and erosion.

All in all, the Northern Plains are a blend of forest and prairie. Varieties of trees, mostly oaks, huddle near the sparkling rivers and cover the backs of the gentle hills. Farther away from the river valleys, prairie grasses stretch for great distances, set off by small clusters of trees.

The western part of the state's central lowlands is formed by the Osage Plains. These plains also stretch into Kansas, Oklahoma, and Texas. Missouri's portion of the Osage Plains features some low hills and wide, shallow valleys that interrupt its flat, even appearance. Because the Osage Plains were glacier-free, the soil there is not as rich. The area is still a productive farming region, though. Coal mining is another important industry in the region.

The Ozark Plateau

The Ozark Plateau makes up the largest part of the state. It covers most of southern Missouri and reaches into Arkansas and Oklahoma. Filled with steep-sloped ridges, deep ravines, and clear, fast-flowing streams, the Ozark Plateau has it all. Low mountains and rugged hills covered with forest add to the region's variety and make it one of the Midwest's most popular vacation spots.

The Ozark Plateau is shaped like a huge dome, or an upside-down bowl. Gently rising, it slowly gains altitude. The highest section is found in the southwest where the land reaches heights of around 1,700 feet (518 m). This part of the plateau extends northeast, ending in the St. Francois Mountains. To the southeast, the Ozark Plateau descends sharply. By the

In Their Own Words

"I have not been on any river that has more of a distinctive personality than does the Missouri River. It's a river that immediately presents to the traveler, 'I am a grandfather spirit. I have a source; I have a life.'"
—William Least Heat-Moon, American writer and historian

MISSOURI

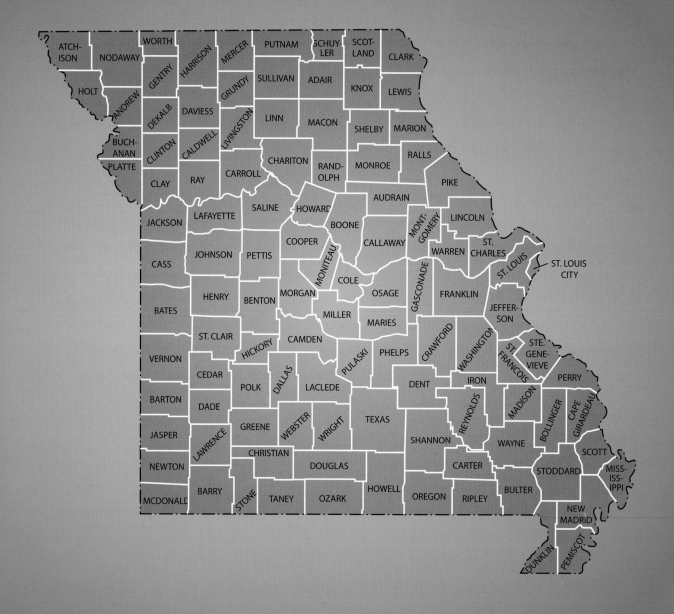

MISSOURI
POPULATION BY COUNTY

County	Population	County	Population	County	Population
Adair	25,607	Grundy	10,261	Perry	18,971
Andrew	17,291	Harrison	8,957	Pettis	42,201
Atchison	5,685	Henry	22,272	Phelps	45,156
Audrain	25,529	Hickory	9,627	Pike	18,516
Barry	35,597	Holt	4,912	Platte	89,322
Barton	12,402	Howard	10,144	Polk	31,137
Bates	17,049	Howell	40,400	Pulaski	52,274
Benton	19,056	Iron	10,630	Putnam	4,979
Bollinger	12,363	Jackson	674,158	Ralls	10,167
Boone	162,642	Jasper	117,404	Randolph	25,414
Buchanan	89,201	Jefferson	218,733	Ray	23,494
Butler	42,794	Johnson	52,595	Reynolds	6,696
Caldwell	9,424	Knox	4,131	Ripley	14,100
Callaway	44,332	Laclede	35,571	St. Charles	360,485
Camden	44,002	Lafayette	33,381	St. Clair	9,805
Cape Girardeau	75,674	Lawrence	38,634	Ste. Genevieve	18,145
Carroll	9,295	Lewis	10,211	St. Francois	65,359
Carter	6,265	Lincoln	52,566	St. Louis	998,954
Cass	99,478	Linn	12,761	St. Louis City	319,294
Cedar	13,982	Livingston	15,195	Saline	23,370
Chariton	7,831	McDonald	23,083	Schuyler	4,431
Christian	77,422	Macon	15,566	Scotland	4,843
Clark	7,139	Madison	12,226	Scott	39,191
Clay	221,939	Maries	9,176	Shannon	8,441
Clinton	20,743	Marion	28,781	Shelby	6,373
Cole	75,990	Mercer	3,785	Stoddard	29,968
Cooper	17,601	Miller	24,748	Stone	32,202
Crawford	24,696	Mississippi	14,358	Sullivan	6,714
Dade	7,883	Moniteau	15,607	Taney	51,675
Dallas	16,777	Monroe	8,840	Texas	26,008
Daviess	8,433	Montgomery	12,236	Vernon	21,159
DeKalb	12,892	Morgan	20,565	Warren	32,513
Dent	15,657	New Madrid	18,956	Washington	25,195
Douglas	13,684	Newton	58,114	Wayne	13,521
Dunklin	31,953	Nodaway	23,370	Webster	36,202
Franklin	101,492	Oregon	10,881	Worth	2,171
Gasconade	15,222	Osage	13,878	Wright	18,815
Gentry	6,738	Ozark	9,723		
Greene	275,174	Pemiscot	18,296		

Source: US Bureau of the Census, 2010

HIGHEST ELEVATION
1772.68 MSL
VERIFIED MARCH 23 1991

MISSOURI

MISSOURI ASSOCIATION OF

REGISTERED LAND SURVEYORS

This plaque verifies that Taum Sauk Mountain is the highest point in Missouri.

time the plateau reaches the plains bordering the Mississippi River, the land is only about 400 feet (122 m) above sea level.

The St. Francois Mountains stretch above the horizon. They are ancient volcanoes that erupted millions of years ago. When this part of the Midwest was covered by water, these mountains probably looked like towering islands rising out of an ancient sea. Today most of the rock found in the rest of the region has been worn away by water and wind. In its place are the rounded domes, spiky knobs, and granite peaks that together cover about 70 square miles (181 square kilometers).

The St. Francois Mountains do not form one continuous chain. Instead, they rise in small groups of usually two to three mountains each. Then the land levels off as it leads to Taum Sauk Mountain, the state's highest point, reaching 1,772 feet (540 m) above sea level.

At one time, millions of years ago, the land stretching across southern Missouri was unbroken. Since then, however, streams have been slicing valleys into the Ozark Plateau. These streams have also shaped much more than the state's surface. Most of the Ozark Plateau is made up of limestone and dolomite. These are two types of rocks formed by layers of tiny particles that are pressed and crushed together. With so many underground rivers in this part of the state, water has slowly eaten away at the layers of rock. Over the years, the running water has sculpted the rock to create a series of fascinating mazes beneath the Show-Me State. Thousands of caves, springs, and sinkholes form Missouri's underground world of wonders.

Missouri is well known for its caves. More than 1,450 of them fan out into long tunnels and magnificent, sprawling caverns. With 10 miles (16 km) of passageways, Marvel Cave, near the city of Branson, is one of the largest. Meramec Caverns in Stanton is another top spot for cave lovers.

Just as impressive are the state's natural springs. Missouri has many **aquifers**, which are underground bodies of water. Springs are formed when pressure from the aquifer forces some of the water to flow to the surface. About ten thousand of these natural springs gurgle and bubble out of the plateau. They are of varying sizes, but many are quite large. More than one hundred springs each give off more than 1 million gallons (3.8 million liters) of water per day. Big Spring, near Van Buren, tops all of them, releasing about 286 million gallons (1.08 billion L) of water each day.

Joining the natural springs in this watery world of southern Missouri are the many **reservoirs** and lakes that dot the Ozark Plateau. The state's second-largest body of water, Lake of the Ozarks, is the crown jewel of southern Missouri. The Lake of the Ozarks was formed when the Bagnell Dam was built across the Osage River in order to generate

One of the features of Marvel Cave near Branson is this flowstone formation called Blondie's Throne.

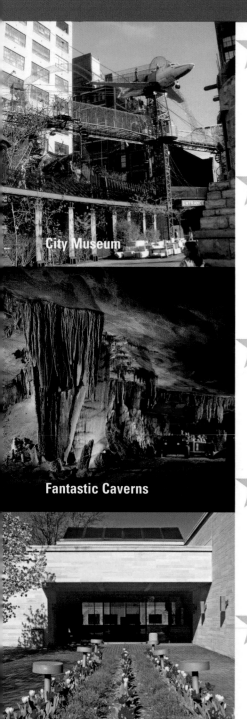

City Museum

Fantastic Caverns

Harry S. Truman Library

1. Bonne Terre Mine

National Geographic calls a tour of Bonne Terre Mine "One of America's Top 10 Greatest Adventures." Founded in 1860, this mine was the world's largest producer of lead ore until it was closed in 1962. The mine includes a 17-mile-long (27 km) lake.

2. City Museum

This children's museum in St. Louis is constructed from reclaimed and recycled materials and is a mixture of children's playground, funhouse, and architectural marvel. Slide down ten-story spiral slides or ride on a 1940s Ferris wheel … on the roof.

3. Fantastic Caverns

America's only ride-through cave, Springfield's Fantastic Caverns was discovered in 1862 by an Ozarks farmer—or more precisely by his dog, who crawled through an entrance. The Cave is toured in jeep-drawn **trams** to preserve its natural features.

4. Gateway Arch

The Gateway Arch is a famous St. Louis structure that symbolizes a "Gateway to the West." Visitors can take an elevator up to a viewing platform at the top, which reaches 625 feet (190.5 m), for stunning views over the city.

5. Harry S. Truman Library

Located in Independence, the Truman Library was the first presidential library created under the 1955 Presidential Libraries Act. It was established to preserve papers, books, and other historical materials relating to former President Harry S. Truman.

MISSOURI ★ ★ ★

6. Mark Twain Boyhood Home and Museum

Famous author Mark Twain lived in this house, built by his father, in Hannibal from ages seven through eighteen. The museum includes photographs, original manuscripts, and the desk at which Twain wrote *The Adventures of Tom Sawyer*.

7. Negro Leagues Baseball Museum

Founded in 1990 in Kansas City, the Negro Leagues Baseball Museum (NLBM) is dedicated to preserving the history of African-American baseball. It includes hundreds of photographs and artifacts dating from the late 1800s through the 1960s.

8. Silver Dollar City

Silver Dollar City in Branson combines a theme park with crafts and the preservation of 1880s Ozark culture. In addition to rides, attractions, and live shows, there are demonstrations of glassblowing, basket weaving, blacksmithing, and pottery and candle making.

9. Trail of Tears State Park

Located in Cape Girardeau County, Trail of Tears State Park marks the place where nine of the thirteen Cherokee Native-American groups being relocated to Oklahoma crossed the Mississippi River during harsh winter conditions in 1838 and 1839.

10. Wilson's Creek National Battlefield

Wilson's Creek was the first major Civil War battle fought west of the Mississippi River. Located in Republic, this is one of the country's best-preserved battlefields. This bloody 1861 Southern victory focused national attention on the war in Missouri.

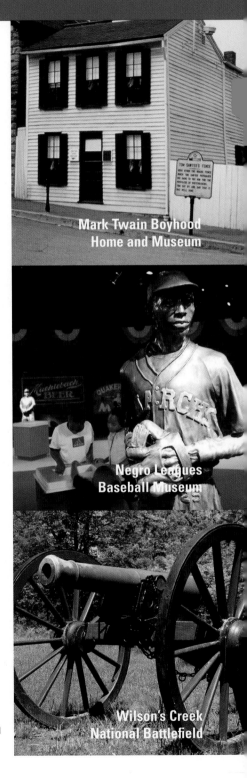

Mark Twain Boyhood Home and Museum

Negro Leagues Baseball Museum

Wilson's Creek National Battlefield

The Lake of the Ozarks formed after the Bagnell Dam was completed. The dam took two years to build.

hydroelectric power (electricity produced by flowing water). The Lake of the Ozarks covers about 55,300 acres (22,379 hectares). Many Missourians love to cruise its waters in their boats. In summer, residents and visitors spend lazy afternoons chugging along, meeting and greeting the other outdoor lovers drawn to this sprawling manmade lake.

The Bootheel

The shape of Missouri looks in some ways like a crooked rectangle, bordered by straight lines and rivers, except for one spot in the southeast where suddenly the state's shape juts down. For such a tiny portion of the state, this region has certainly earned a lot of names. When most Missourians refer to the region, they simply call it the Bootheel. It gets its name from its shape, which resembles the thick heel of a cowboy boot. The area is also called the southeastern lowlands or the gulf coastal plains.

The Bootheel actually forms the northernmost part of the Mississippi Alluvial Plain, which stretches across parts of seven states, from southern Louisiana to southern Illinois. The word alluvial refers to all the sand, silt, minerals, and nutrients that Mississippi floodwaters leave behind each year. Because of all these rich deposits, this is the most fertile part of Missouri. It is also the flattest, with a few low ridges breaking up the landscape here and there.

Severe winter weather is rare in Missouri, but snow does make a rare appearance.

Before settlers arrived, the Bootheel was covered in water that surrounded the dense, swampy forests. Through the years, settlers cleared and drained the area and turned it into a prime farming region. Today cotton, soybeans, corn, and rice thrive in the area.

Climate

As native Missourians often say, "If you don't like the weather, wait an hour, and it'll change."

Missouri has a variable climate, meaning it is subject to a range of temperatures. In the hilly or mountainous areas, winters and summers tend to be milder than in regions with lower elevations. Residents in the southeast can expect about 50 inches (127 centimeters) of precipitation per year. Precipitation is all the moisture that falls, usually in the form of rain and snow.

Digging In His Heels

The unusual shape of Missouri's "bootheel" came about because of one farmer. John Hardeman Walker owned most of the land there. When Missouri explored becoming a state, Walker realized that the proposed boundary would have left his property in Arkansas. He used his power to influence the government to include his property in Missouri.

Deadly Storm

The most destructive US tornado on record occurred in Annapolis, Missouri. In three hours, it tore through the town on March 18, 1925, leaving a 980-foot- [299 m] wide trail of demolished buildings, uprooted trees, and overturned cars. It left 823 people dead and almost three thousand injured.

Missourians who live in the northwest receive far less precipitation, with about 30 inches (76 cm) per year.

Summers in the state tend to be long, warm and humid, with the sticky weather sometimes lasting from June to September. The highest temperature ever recorded in the state is 118 degrees Fahrenheit (47.8° Celsius). This mark was hit three different times, on July 15 and 18, 1936, and on July 14, 1954.

Winters are both brief and unpredictable. They are rarely severe and may even feature brief periods of warmth. In the middle of winter, it is not uncommon to have pleasant days when the temperature reaches between 50°F and 60°F (10 and 15.5°C). These patches of warmth can just as easily be followed by periods of severe cold. The state's record low temperature is –40°F (–40°C), recorded in Warsaw on February 13, 1905.

Severe Weather Is a Threat

The variation in Missouri's climate can sometimes lead to violent and even deadly storms. Air masses of different temperatures often clash over Missouri during spring, especially in April and May, as remnants of winter do not want to let go, and summer heat is just around the corner. Severe thunderstorms, which can bring flooding rains, damaging hail, and strong winds, are common during this transition season.

Tornadoes are even more terrifying and often associated with severe thunderstorms. Missouri recorded forty-nine tornadoes in 2013. On average, the Show-Me State experiences just over thirty tornadoes a year, with about half of them occurring during April and May. On May 22, 2011, a powerful tornado with a **funnel** nearly 1 mile (1.6 km) wide tore through the town of Joplin. More than one thousand people were injured and 158 were killed.

Wild Missouri

Forests cover about one-third of Missouri. They are generally found in the southern part of the state and in the river valleys of the north. A majority of the Show-Me State's trees, mostly hardwoods, come from the oak and hickory families. Sweet gum, bald cypress, cottonwoods, elms, and maples are present in large numbers, too.

In springtime, the Ozark Plateau is a wildflower paradise. Flowers native to the state include violets, anemones, buttercups, wild roses, phlox, asters, columbines, and goldenrods, to name just a few. A short walk through any of Missouri's wild stretches will reveal many more.

With so much variety in its terrain, it is not surprising that the state is home to a wide range of animals. In the state's forests and along its grassy plains, cottontail rabbits, beavers, foxes, squirrels, raccoons, and opossums all share the land's resources. White-tailed deer sneak out of the cover of trees to munch grass in the fields.

Birds are also drawn to Missouri's mild climate and to the food the wilderness provides. Mockingbirds, purple finches, woodpeckers, and blue jays fill the air with their songs. They nest in the trees and shrubs that grow across the state.

With 56,000 miles (90,123 km) of streams within its borders, Missouri's waterways are filled with fish. Bass, bluegills, catfish, crappies, and trout add to the aquatic variety, much to the joy of many state residents. Missouri is fishing country. Bass Pro Shop, a fishing and outdoor recreation retailer, has its headquarters in Springfield.

Though Missourians take great care of their state, many of its animals have been threatened through the years. With the spread of suburbs and more and more land being developed, some animals were losing their homes. State scientists and officials became concerned when population levels for these animals started to decline. They came up with a plan to reverse this trend, and so far their efforts have paid off. State conservation workers have been successful in building up Missouri's population of once-threatened species such as white-tailed deer, wild turkeys, and otters. These are just three of the success stories, but they serve as proof of Missourians' love for their state and their desire to be sure that all its residents—both human and nonhuman—thrive.

Development has threatened the homes of animals who live in Missouri's forests.

10 KEY PLANTS AND ANIMALS

Armadillo

Channel Catfish

1. Armadillo

Missouri has a small but growing population of these animals. About the size of a housecat and with a tough, protective shell, armadillos frustrate homeowners by digging up their yards to find invertebrates like insects and worms in the soil.

2. Channel Catfish

The channel catfish is the official state fish. Slender with a forked tail, the species uses its catlike whiskers to feel out a possible meal. Adults can grow to 32 inches (81 cm) long and weigh 15 pounds (6.8 kilograms).

3. Chiggers

The worst thing about Missouri summers is chiggers. These insects are extremely tiny, and you need a hand lens or microscope to see them well. Their presence is best known, instead, by the intensely itchy welts their bites leave behind.

4. Crayfish

Missouri has at least thirty-five species of crayfish. Crayfish often appear in densities of around twenty animals per square meter of stream surface area, greater than almost anywhere else in the world. Crayfish are an important food for animals and humans.

5. Elk

A very large member of the deer family, elk are brown or tan with a yellowish-brown rump patch and tail. Plentiful before European settlement, elk had disappeared from Missouri by 1865. In 2010, Missouri's Department of Conservation began restoring elk to Missouri.

Crayfish

6. Grapes

Missouri's warm summers and rocky soil are perfect for grape growing. Though they can be eaten off the vine, grapes are often used to make wine. Missouri's wine industry was started by Germans who immigrated to the territory in the early 1800s.

7. Missouri Gooseberry

This shrub grows mostly in moist, wooded ravines. Its greenish-white flowers appear in March or April, after which berries dot the bush from June to September. Missouri cooks use juicy gooseberries to make delicious jams and jellies.

8. Mushrooms

Mushrooms are neither plants nor animals. They constitute their own scientific classification—Fungi. There are about ten thousand kinds of mushrooms in North America, and many can be found in Missouri. Many mushrooms are delicious and nutritious, but others can be poisonous!

9. Ozark Zigzag Salamander

The Ozark Zigzag Salamander is found only in the southern Missouri Ozarks. It burrows under moist leaves or rotting logs and may be red-striped, yellow-striped, or unstriped. They do not have lungs. They absorb oxygen through their skin and mouths.

10. Pawpaw

Sometimes called "Missouri's banana," pawpaws are small trees that produce fruit that is cylindrical and oblong. The green skin of the unripe fruit turns yellow as it matures. Once ripe, the fruit becomes edible and has a banana-like taste.

Grapes

Ozark Zigzag Salamander

Pawpaw

Evidence of life among the Paleo-Indians can be found at the Mastodon State Historic Site. Included is a skeleton of the large animal for which the site is named.

From the Beginning

Nomadic hunters first wandered Missouri in search of game about twelve thousand years ago. Called Paleo-Indians, these people were the ancestors of the Native Americans who would eventually spread across North America. Paleo means older or ancient. The Paleo-Indians camped in simple, short-term shelters while hunting or searching for food.

For many years, very little was known about the Paleo-Indians. Scientists have only recently been able to piece together a more complete picture of Paleo-Indian life. One important discovery was the Kimmswick Bone Bed at Mastodon State Historic Site, in Imperial. The site has offered some valuable artifacts. Clovis points, which are a kind of spear tip, and other stone tools were found along with the remains of a mastodon, a huge prehistoric creature that was often hunted. The site offered the first proof that mastodons had lived during the time of the Paleo-Indians. Valuable finds such as these provide an important glimpse into a mysterious and far-distant past.

By 3000 BCE Missouri's early residents were making baskets and had developed a variety of stone tools. Pottery was introduced to the region, followed by an even more important addition—agriculture. Farming meant that people could settle into more permanent villages and establish more stable lives.

The Native Past

After the Paleo-Indians, another group of people, called the Mound Builders, settled in the region. These people rose to power along the Mississippi River valley. Today, there are traces of their once-bustling urban center, Cahokia, just across the Mississippi River in west-central Illinois. Experts estimate that Cahokia had a population of about twenty thousand around the year 1100 CE. In the center of the city stood a huge flat-topped mound standing almost 100 feet (30.5 m) tall. Experts believe it and the other mounds were used for burial and religious purposes and to mark important locations. The mounds might have also been used for other reasons. As many as one hundred mounds have been found in the area.

The culture of the Mound Builders gave rise to the various Native American groups that were well established in the region by the time the first European explorers arrived. Missouri's forests and prairies were filled with game, and the state offered an ideal place for these native communities to thrive. The early Native Americans spent roughly half of the year following herds of animals. The other half of the year, they settled in simple villages where they grew a variety of vegetables.

The largest and most powerful group in the region was the Osage. Today the Osage River bears their name and marks the spot where this strong nation settled. The Osage lived in the south and west of Missouri in villages made up of cone-shaped huts. Larger buildings, for meetings and ceremonies, were made of poles woven together with long strands of grass. The Osage were hunters and farmers and took advantage of all Missouri had to offer. Deer, bison, and bear were just some of the animals they hunted in the wilds of Missouri. Their gardens were filled with pumpkins, corn, beans, and squash.

Other groups shared the region as well. The Otoe lived north of the Missouri River. The Missouri (or Missouria) settled mostly in the eastern and central portions of the state. The name "Missouri" comes from a word from the Siouan language, which was spoken

Three Osage men, He Who Takes Away, War, and Mink-chesk, were painted in 1834. Their tribe was eventually driven out of Missouri.

by Native American tribes from the Great Plains and the south of Canada. It comes from the tribal name Missouria, which means "big canoe people." The Missouria called themselves Niuachi, meaning: "People of the river's mouth."

Around 1790, a group of Shawnee **migrated** west of the Mississippi River and settled near Cape Girardeau. By 1815, more than 1,200 Shawnee lived there. They were soon joined by a large band of Delaware Native Americans, and the two groups became closely linked. Although the Osage dominated the region for years, the Iowa, and later the Sac and Fox, became powerful in the early 1800s.

Europeans Arrive

French explorers Jacques Marquette and Louis Jolliet were most likely the first Europeans to reach the mouth of the Missouri River. In 1673, they marked the spot where the Big Muddy pours into the Mississippi. They met the Peoria, a native group that offered the hungry explorers food and shelter on their long journey.

Hunters and trappers moved into Missouri along its rivers, which made travel easier.

The Native People

Native Americans roamed the area we now call Missouri long before Europeans arrived in the new world. While the name "Missouri" comes from the language of the Missouria tribe, other native people living there included the Chickasaw, Illini, Ioway, Osage, Otoe, and Quapaw. The Osage tribe, part of the Great Sioux Nation, occupied areas south of the Missouri River, spreading into northern Arkansas and northeast Oklahoma. Only the Osage Native Americans seemed to be native to Missouri and the Ozark region. All the other tribes had been driven from east of the Mississippi River as Europeans made a gradual advance across the eastern portion of North America. The warlike Osage had enough warriors to rule this area against the other tribes that flanked them on every side.

Native Americans during this period were nomadic, moving from area to area, living in tepees based on weather and the availability of food. They also farmed for six months of the year, harvesting corn, beans, and squash near their villages. They had no horses, cattle, sheep, or guns. The Europeans brought those things.

As more Europeans arrived in America, other tribes migrated into Missouri, mostly due to the government's Native American removal policy. These included the Cherokee, Delaware, Kickapoo, Shawnee, and Sac and Fox tribes. These movements put pressure on

The Fox and the Sac arrived in Missouri in the early 1800s after being driven out of their lands around the Great Lakes.

tribes already living there, causing wars and weakening all the tribes. Between 1803 and 1825, the Osage were forced to sign treaties with the government. These treaties took all of their land and made them move to a **reservation** along the Kansas border.

Most Native Americans were forced to leave Missouri during the 1800s, moving to reservations in Oklahoma. Today there are only about twenty-seven thousand Native Americans living in Missouri, about 0.5 percent of the population. There are no federally recognized Native American tribes or any tribal reservations in Missouri today. There are still some Native Americans from the Cherokee Nation living in the state. They are descendants of people who were able to break away from other tribes while being forced to march through Missouri during the Trail of Tears.

Spotlight on the the Osage

Osage is pronounced "oh-sage" in English, but when Native Americans say it in their own language, they pronounce it similar to "wah-zah-zhay." The Osage are original people of Missouri, Oklahoma, Kansas, and Arkansas, but they were forced to move to reservations in Kansas and then Oklahoma during the early 1800s. Most Osage people still live in Oklahoma.

Homes: Most Osage Native Americans lived in settled villages of round earthen lodges. Osage lodges were made from wooden frames covered with packed earth.

Government: The Osage live on a reservation in Oklahoma today, which is land that belongs to them and is under their control. The Osage Nation has its own government, laws, police, and services, just like a small country. The Osage chief is elected by all the tribal members. However, the Osage are also US citizens and must obey American law.

Clothing: Osage women wore long deerskin dresses and leggings, which they decorated with fancy beadwork and ribbons. Osage men wore breechcloths with leather leggings. The Osage wore moccasins on their feet, and in cold weather they wore long buffalo-hide robes.

Language: The Osage people speak English today. Only a few Osage people, mostly elders, still speak their native Osage language. However, some young Osage Native Americans are working to learn their ancient language again.

Food: The Osage Native Americans were big game hunters. They especially liked to hunt buffalo. Osage women worked together to raise crops of corn, beans, squash, and pumpkins.

Crafts: Osage artists are famous for their woodcarving and beadwork.

Other curious explorers soon followed Marquette and Jolliet. In 1682, fellow Frenchman René-Robert Cavelier Sieur de La Salle traveled down the Mississippi River. He declared the entire valley the property of the French government. He and other early explorers spoke of the natural resources that Missouri and the entire midwestern region held.

Eight Is Enough

Tennessee and Missouri are the only two states that share their borders with eight other states. No other state has more close neighbors.

Some of these early adventurers were lured with tales of gold and silver lying just beneath the surface. While French miners never found these valuable metals, they did uncover lead and salt. Their efforts were mostly focused in what is now St. Francois County, where they set up a successful operation.

Trappers were also drawn to the region. They arrived and took advantage of the wealth of furbearing animals that lived in Missouri. Trade routes were set up, and soon trading posts dotted the Mississippi River valley. Large quantities of furs were sent downriver and on to the East Coast and Europe. Missouri's location near two major waterways supported the shipment of goods and helped to speed the gradual settlement of the area.

Missionaries came as well, eager to convert the Native Americans to Catholicism. They set up several missions in the area. Around 1700, Jesuit missionaries set up Missouri's first European settlement at the Mission of St. Francis Xavier. It stood near present-day St. Louis. However, the nearby swamps posed too many threats. Disease spread easily through the mission, and the site was left behind in 1703.

The area's first permanent European settlement was founded around 1750. Settlers from Illinois crossed into Missouri and set up a small community at Sainte Genevieve. They were mostly French miners drawn to the area's rich deposits of lead. These miners opened the door for a string of larger and more successful communities to come. In 1764, Pierre Laclède and thirteen-year-old Auguste Chouteau founded St. Louis. The future city served as a trading post and as the base for their new fur empire. Avenues and districts in St. Louis still bear their names today.

While the French were the dominant European influence at that time, Missouri was about to change hands. In a 1762 treaty, France gave all of its lands west of the Mississippi River to Spain, and Missouri became a Spanish colony. The Spaniards wanted to see their new territory prosper. They encouraged settlers from the eastern portion of the continent

Daniel Boone and much of his extended family moved into Missouri in 1799. He lived the last twenty years of his life in the region.

to move in and tame the unclaimed wilderness. Hundreds of new settlers came from Kentucky, Tennessee, Virginia, and the Carolinas.

Among the newcomers was legendary frontiersman Daniel Boone. He arrived at St. Charles County in 1799 after the Spanish had given him 850 acres (344 ha) of land. In 1800, Boone became a syndic, or frontier judge, in the area. He grew to love his adopted state and considered himself a Missourian for the rest of his life.

Spain's control of the territory was to be short-lived. Missouri changed ownership again in 1800. France, under its leader Napoléon Bonaparte, demanded the valuable territory back from Spain. So the frontier residents once again came under French rule. By then, most of Missouri had been thoroughly explored. Communities had begun to spring up across the region.

As war raged back in Europe, Napoléon and his nation were in need of money. The French leader unhappily sold the region to the United States in 1803. As part of what is known as the Louisiana Purchase, Missouri officially changed hands for its third and final time. The vast territory was divided into two parts. Missouri was included in the northern part, referred to as Upper Louisiana.

The New Territory

Congress officially made Missouri a territory in 1812. At the time, its population totaled about twenty thousand. Unlike other territories, Missouri already had its own bustling economy. Farmers harvested crops. Miners removed valuable ores and minerals from the rich earth. Prosperous communities continued to grow, building schools and adding churches. Word spread quickly, and many settlers were convinced that Missouri was the perfect place to live. Even more people poured into the region. The new arrivals helped the

Making Walnut Shell Turtles

Missouri's state reptile is the three-toed box turtle. The state nut is the black walnut. You can use walnut shells to make a family of turtles!

What You Need

One black walnut (regular walnuts will do) for every two turtles. Because the shells sometimes break, have some extra walnuts handy.

Card stock (any color)

Green and other colors of construction paper

Glue, scissors, and thin string (optional)

What To Do

- Crack the walnuts in half and remove the nuts from the shell.
- Next place the shell on the card stock and draw a body, making 4 legs, a head, and tail. Cut out and use this as a stencil.
- Trace the stencil on the construction paper, making as many as you want. You can make them all different colors or all the same—whatever you prefer.
- When all the bodies are traced, add glue to your shells.
- Place the shells on the bodies and let the glue dry.
- Draw eyes on the head and three toes on each foot.
- Cut out the bodies when all glue is dry.
- To turn your turtle into an ornament, punch a small hole in the nose, loop string through it and tie the end.

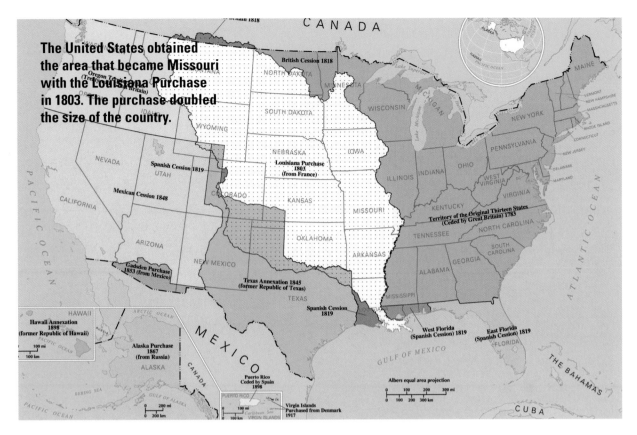

The United States obtained the area that became Missouri with the Louisiana Purchase in 1803. The purchase doubled the size of the country.

territory to grow and thrive all the more. Kansas City emerged as a new urban community as well as a center for the state's grain and livestock markets.

Pioneers also settled in Missouri's Ozark Mountains. Many came from southern states. They settled the Ozark region, building homesteads and establishing small farms and communities. Ozark residents established mills on the river and found ways to survive in the rugged terrain.

Not all the residents of the territory were happy about the growing population, however. With so many new arrivals, competition for land increased. Soon the area's many Native Americans were being pushed off the lands they and their ancestors had called home for hundreds of years. The territory's Native Americans were slowly forced to move their homes farther west. Conflicts arose as some native groups decided to resist, launching a series of raids on the frontier settlements.

Around the same time, the War of 1812 had broken out between the United States and Great Britain. In an effort to gain support and to weaken the Americans, the British gave weapons to the Native Americans. They also encouraged them to continue their attacks. The settlers responded by building more forts and making existing structures even stronger.

When the War of 1812 came to an end, all tensions did not end with it. Native Americans continued their raids into 1815, until a treaty signed at Portage des Sioux

Churning butter, hunting, and playing games were a part of life on the frontier.

ended the fighting and took away more traditional Native-American lands. It was a sign of things to come. By the following year, only five thousand Native Americans were left in the state. By 1825, the Osage had given up all of their Missouri holdings and moved to Kansas. By the late 1830s, most of the state's Native Americans had been killed, driven away, or forced onto reservations in neighboring states.

Memorable Words

No one knows for sure who first called Missouri the "Show-Me State," but many believe it was Missouri's US Congressman Willard Duncan Vandiver. During a speech, Vandiver said, "Frothy eloquence neither convinces nor satisfies me. I am from Missouri. You have got to show me."

The Great Compromise

Missouri leaders asked the US Congress to make the territory a state in 1818. The request brought a serious problem to Missouri that would divide it for many years to come.

In its early days, the region had been mostly settled by Southerners who had brought their **slaves** with them. These settlers wanted to continue to own slaves as Missouri applied for statehood. At that time, however, there was a growing movement in the United States to end slavery, or at least to forbid it in new states as they were added to the Union. When Missourians asked to be admitted to the Union as a slave state, one that permitted slavery, the request heated up a growing nationwide debate. Many people in the rest of the nation wanted Missouri to be a free state, where slavery would not be allowed.

The dispute was not decided until 1820, when Congress adopted the Missouri Compromise. Under its terms, Missouri would be admitted as a slave state if Maine entered as a free state. The plan would maintain the balance between free and slave states in the US Congress. Neither side, those for and against slavery, would have the greater power. Also, no state except Missouri above latitude 36°30', which is Missouri's southern border, could have slaves. So, on August 10, 1821, Missouri officially became the twenty-fourth state. At the time, the new state had a population of 66,586 people, including its 10,222 slaves.

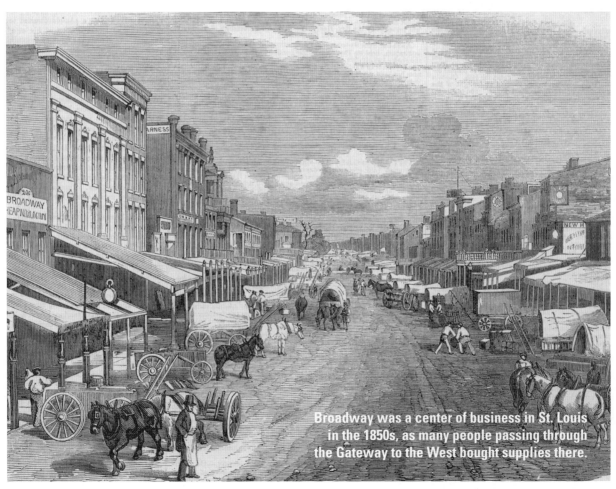

Broadway was a center of business in St. Louis in the 1850s, as many people passing through the Gateway to the West bought supplies there.

★ 10 ★ KEY CITIES ★

Kansas City

St. Louis

1. Kansas City: population 459,787

Settled in the early 1800s as a port on the Missouri River, Kansas City is known as the "City of Fountains," with more than 250 fountains around town. It is located near the geographic center of the United States.

2. St. Louis: population 319,294

Situated where the Mississippi and Missouri Rivers meet, St. Louis has developed into a national hub for business, culture, and recreation. Not far from St. Louis's urban core are the beautiful rolling hills of the Ozark Mountain region.

3. Springfield: population 159,498

Known as "The Queen City of the Ozarks" because of its location on the Ozark Plateau, Springfield is home to Missouri State University. It is recognized as the birthplace of Route 66, the country's first paved transcontinental highway.

4. Independence: population 116,830

Part of the greater Kansas City area, Independence was founded in 1827 and grew rapidly as a trading post. Known as the "Queen City of the Trails," Independence was a point of departure for the California, Oregon, and Santa Fe Trails.

5. Columbia: population 108,500

Founded in 1819, Columbia lies in the heart of the state, right between Kansas City—127 miles (204 km) to the west—and St. Louis—124 miles (199.5 km) to the east. Columbia is home to the University of Missouri as well as Columbia and Stephens Colleges.

6. ## Lee's Summit: population 91,364

The area around Lee's Summit was a beautiful prairie inhabited by Osage Native Americans. Located close to Kansas City, Lee's Summit has been named one of the country's top places to live several times by *Money* magazine.

7. ## O'Fallon: population 79,329

A small town until the mid-1970s, O'Fallon grew quickly by expanding its business and tourism attractions. Just minutes west of St. Louis, O'Fallon was also named one of America's best places to live by *Money* magazine in 2014.

8. ## St. Joseph: population 76,780

Located a half-hour from Kansas City, St. Joseph was established in 1843 as a trading post. The Pony Express was launched from St. Joseph on April 3, 1860, and famous outlaw Jesse James was killed there in 1882.

9. ## St. Charles: population 65,794

Saint Charles has been welcoming visitors to its river shore since 1769. Visitors can still enjoy the sights and sounds of early America by strolling along the brick-paved streets of Missouri's oldest and largest historic district.

10. ## St. Peters: population 52,575

St. Peters is a growing community situated less than 30 miles (48 km) from downtown St. Louis. It is home to the Rec-Plex, a huge workout facility with ice rinks, swimming and diving pools, and much more.

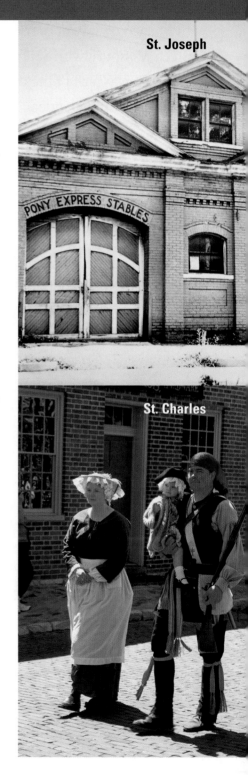

St. Joseph

St. Charles

The Gateway

Missouri will long be remembered for the important role it played in the settling of the western frontier. The state was considered a starting point where many western expeditions were launched. For years the territory had been conducting a growing trade with Mexico by way of the Santa Fe Trail. This important route linked Independence, in western Missouri, with Santa Fe. Today, Santa Fe is in the US state of New Mexico, but at that time it was part of the country of Mexico.

The city of Independence became one of the leading economic centers on the frontier. Soon the Oregon Trail, which took settlers to the Pacific Northwest, also became a heavily traveled route. The Oregon Trail also started in the prosperous city of Independence. All this activity spelled greater growth for the state. By 1860, Missouri had 1.2 million residents—eighteen times the number of people the state claimed in 1820.

Thomas Hart Benton served five terms as a senator from Missouri. He did not want slavery to expand into the territories.

The Road to War

When the Missouri Compromise was agreed to in 1820, people hoped that the controversy over the issue of slavery would eventually calm. By keeping the number of slave states and free states equal at that time, many believe the Missouri Compromise at least delayed the start of what would become the Civil War. However, Thomas Jefferson once wrote that dividing the country in such a way would cause the destruction of the Union. While the compromise kept the balance intact, it did nothing to settle the differences between those who supported slavery and those who wanted it abolished.

These tensions hit home most noticeably in the western part of Missouri. Some Missourians living in the area feared that the Kansas Territory, right over the border, would be admitted to the Union as a free state. Many antislavery supporters had moved to Kansas, and they were determined to keep Kansas slavery-free. Tensions along the Missouri–Kansas border became so high that violence soon erupted. In 1854, the Kansas-Nebraska Act was passed. It repealed the

Missouri Compromise and said that Kansas and Nebraska had the right to choose if they were going to be free or slave states, even though they were above latitude 36°30'. The US Supreme Court declared the Missouri Compromise unconstitutional in 1857. Fighting and skirmishes would continue to grip the region until the end of the Civil War (1861–1865), despite the fact that Kansas was admitted to the Union in 1861 as a free state.

Fifty-Year Beard

When Abraham Lincoln ran for president, a Missourian named Valentine Tapley from Pike County swore that he would never shave again if Abe were elected. Tapley kept his word and his beard was more than 12 feet [3.64 m] long when he died in 1910.

Though Missouri was a slave state, its officials were unsure what course the state would take when the Civil War began and divided the nation. Southern supporters wondered if the state would secede, or withdraw, from the Union and become a part of the Confederate States of America, the name for the group of Southern states that fought against the North. Others wanted the state to abandon slavery and stay in the Union. Many Missourians did not want to choose sides at all.

Officials forced the issue, though. The pro-Southern governor at the time, Claiborne F. Jackson, held a state **convention** to find out what plan of action Missourians wanted to adopt. After a series of meetings in February and March 1861, the members of the convention voted to remain part of the Union. Missourians wanted the fighting to stay as far away from their state as possible. This wish eventually proved impossible.

Missourians' hopes for peace at home did not last long. When President Abraham Lincoln asked Missouri to send troops to fight for the North, Governor Jackson refused. The governor was commander of the state militia, which clashed with Union troops at Boonville on June 17, 1861. The Union troops, under the command of General Nathaniel Lyon, defeated the governor's troops and seized control of northern Missouri. Meanwhile, Jackson and his supporters regrouped in the southwestern part of the state. They then marched to Wilson's Creek near Springfield where, with the help of Confederate troops, they defeated the Union forces.

Ulysses S. Grant was living in Missouri at the time. After his graduation from West Point, Grant had been stationed in Missouri. He met his future wife there and married her after the Mexican War. He resigned from the army in 1854 to become a farmer in the state. At the start of the Civil War, he returned to the army and eventually was in charge of

Confederate forces controlled key positions at Pea Ridge, Arkansas, on March 7, 1862. The next day, the Union Army turned the tide. The victory put Missouri under Union control.

Swift Justice

In 1865, Missouri became the first slave state to free its slaves.

the winning Union forces. He then served two terms as president of the United States.

The start of the Civil War had only divided the state even more. To try and remedy this, another state political convention was held. Officials decided to remove pro-Confederate leaders from office and replace them with individuals loyal to the Union cause. To begin the process, a new governor, Hamilton R. Gamble, was chosen.

Former Governor Jackson did not step down quietly, however. In October 1861, Jackson called a meeting of the state legislature at Neosho. Not enough legislators attended to make the meeting official, but those who did come decided to secede from the Union. As a result, the state became physically as well as politically divided. Confederate forces controlled southern portions of the state, while northern parts remained loyal to the Union.

In March 1862, Union troops reclaimed the southern area after winning a battle in nearby Pea Ridge, Arkansas. During another Confederate attempt to recapture Missouri, Southern soldiers were soundly defeated in 1864 near Kansas City. That battle marked the official end of fighting between the Northern and Southern armies in Missouri. However, the rivalry and division did not go away. Small bands of pro-North and pro-South supporters would continue to engage in combat until the end of the war. Roving groups also wandered across the countryside, burning and looting towns and killing people whom they thought were disloyal to their cause.

Boom Towns

The war years marked a major change for the state in several ways. Despite the deep political divisions the state faced, Missouri thrived and continued to build its economy. Soon after the war, St. Louis and Kansas City became major business centers.

As trade along the Santa Fe Trail ended and the fur trade declined, the state's economy was forced to shift. Business leaders began looking to new sources of income. They also realized it was cheaper to process raw materials in Missouri than pay the costs to ship them to processors in the East. Soon, flour and lumber mills sprang up. By the 1860s, St. Louis was producing about 500,000 barrels (578,140,000 L) of flour per year. Beef, corn, oats, and apples were also processed and shipped out of the state. Factories made cloth,

One Scoop or Two?

The ice cream cone was invented at the St. Louis World's Fair in 1904 when an ice cream vendor ran out of cups and asked a waffle vendor to help by rolling up waffles to hold ice cream.

Temporary camps were set up to house workers as they laid tracks for the railroad.

Life was hard for the families of sharecroppers. This girl was photographed in 1938 in her family's cabin in New Madrid County.

and iron and lead products, while breweries produced beer.

Transportation routes improved slowly but steadily. By 1870, there were about 2,000 miles (3,219 km) of railroad tracks crisscrossing Missouri. Soon **immigrants** from places like Germany, Ireland, and Italy flocked into the state. The face of Missouri was once again changing.

Reform

The first decade of the twentieth century brought about a call for reform and statewide improvements to make life better and safer for all the state's residents. Governor Joseph W. Folk took office in 1905. During his term, new laws were passed to change how elections were run and how the state did business. Another change meant Missouri's factories were to be inspected to make sure employees were given fair working conditions. Laws controlling child labor and the state's public utilities were also passed. Schools were improved, and the prison system was reformed. The state's systems of highways and roads were also expanded and improved.

War gripped the nation once again as it entered World War I in 1917. While the price to the nation was high in terms of death and suffering, World War I actually helped boost Missouri's industries. Miners, factory workers, and farmers all increased production to make needed supplies for the American troops. General John J. Pershing, who was born in Linn County, was chosen to head the nation's troops in France. He became just one of thousands of Missourians fighting in the war overseas.

While Missouri boomed after World War I, the arrival of the Great Depression proved a major setback for the state. During the 1930s, Missourians faced hard times. Many lost their jobs, and families struggled to make ends meet. Low crop prices spelled disaster for

At a tractorette school in Maryville in 1942, women learned how to use farm machinery so they could grow food for the troops during World War II.

countless farmers. The state government cut jobs and laid off workers in an attempt to save money. Relief came from federal programs. Agencies were set up to give people jobs building dams, bridges, and roads, and improving public lands.

World War II and Beyond

In the 1940s, another World War gave Missouri's struggling economy the jolt it needed. New industries were developed to supply the United States' armed forces fighting in Europe and Asia.

In 1944, Harry Truman, a US senator from Independence, was elected Vice President. When President Franklin D. Roosevelt died in office in 1945, Truman stepped into the role of President. He was elected to a full term in 1948.

The 1950s saw another important shift in the state's economy. New factories and industrial plants opened across the state as Missouri enjoyed its postwar prosperity. However, new challenges were in store for both the state's cities and farms.

Starting in the early 1970s, many of Missouri's urban residents began fleeing to the suburbs, taking their tax dollars with them. This meant there was less money available for the inner cities. Crime was on the rise as well. Stretches of St. Louis began to look like a ghost town. Buildings became neglected and were in need of repair. Once again, the cities were facing a turning point.

In Their Own Words

"If you can't stand the heat, get out of the kitchen."
—Harry S. Truman, US president

Those living in rural areas faced their own trials as well. During the 1980s, Missouri continued to lose its farms at an alarming rate. Farms proved too difficult—and expensive—for many families to maintain.

Despite these problems, the 1990s were a time of rebuilding and economic growth. Cities formed plans to rebuild their downtown areas and to encourage new businesses. While farming declined, resourceful Missourians once again found new ways of earning an income.

Today, Missouri stands firmly committed to improving schools, protecting the environment, and building its economy. Despite the setbacks, farming and farm products still play an important role in the state's economy. New businesses and industries have moved into the state as well. Missourians know that if they remain strong and are able to change with the times, they can look to the future with confidence, proud to live in their beloved Show-Me State.

10 KEY DATES IN STATE HISTORY

1. 12,000 BCE

The Paleo-Indians roam the area now called Missouri, hunting mastodons for meat and the giant ground sloth for fur.

2. June 25, 1673

Explorers Jacques Marquette and Louis Jolliet meet Illinois Native Americans in northeast Missouri at what is now Iliniwek Village State Historic Site.

3. June 4, 1812

A portion of the Territory of Louisiana becomes the Territory of Missouri. The new territory included present-day Arkansas until they split in 1819.

4. March 3, 1820

Congress passed "the Missouri Compromise," allowing slavery in Missouri but not in the rest of the Louisiana Purchase north of the thirty-sixth parallel.

5. August 10, 1821

Missouri is admitted to the Union as the twenty-fourth state after the Missouri Compromise satisfied those in Congress who were for, and those who were against, slavery.

6. June 2, 1825

The Osage Native Americans turn the last of their lands over to the United States government and move west to a reservation in Kansas.

7. April 3, 1860

The Pony Express service officially begins when men riding horses, carrying saddlebags of mail, leave simultaneously from St. Joseph, Missouri, and Sacramento, California.

8. August 6, 1929

Construction begins on the Bagnell Dam on the Osage River. The dam created the Lake of the Ozarks and was completed in 1931.

9. May 22, 2011

The deadliest tornado to strike the United States in sixty years occurs in Joplin. The tornado kills 158 people and injures more than 1,000.

10. August 9, 2014

Unarmed black teenager Michael Brown is shot and killed in Ferguson by a white police officer, sparking protests and discussions about race relations across the country.

A statue of the beloved St. Louis Cardinal Stan Musial stands outside of the new Busch Stadium, which opened in 2006 (the old Busch Stadium closed in 2005).

The People

3

S ince its earliest days, Missouri has been a blend of cultures and ethnic traditions. Most of the state's initial settlers were American-born families of Scots-Irish, English, Welsh, German, Dutch, and Swedish descent. From the 1830s to the 1860s, Missouri's population almost doubled with every decade.

Most of the newcomers had been born in America, but many others came from Germany, Ireland, Italy, and other European nations. By 1842, St. Louis was home to an Orthodox Jewish community of about one hundred people. One historian believes this group can be traced back to Poland, Bohemia, and possibly England. The end of the 1800s brought even more new faces to the state. Missouri became a melting pot of people from different cultures, searching for better lives. The trend continues to this day.

Native Americans

Though Native Americans once made up the largest population in the state, today their numbers are far smaller. The most recent census showed that only about one-half of one percent of the population is Native American. Though that accounts for just a tiny portion of the state's residents, Missouri's Native Americans are still a strong presence. Throughout the year, many observe traditional holidays and events. Across the state,

A small remnant of the Native American population celebrates its heritage in Missouri.

Up From Slavery

Blanche Kelso Bruce was the son of a Mississippi slave and a slave himself. He became the first African American to serve a full term in the US Senate starting in 1875, and he founded a school for blacks in Hannibal.

several Native American groups hold festivals and other celebrations honoring their history and heritage.

A European Mix

Descendants of Missouri's German immigrants make up the largest ethnic group living in the state today. A German presence can be felt in pockets across the state, especially in towns such as Hermann to the west of St. Louis. Many German settlers came to this part of the state and spread out along the Missouri River valley.

Some immigrants sought out this area of the state because it reminded them of their homeland, in particular the stately Rhine River valley. Just like in that region of Germany, a winemaking industry quickly developed in Missouri's "Little Rhine" region. This was just one of the many traditions and pursuits the German settlers brought with them.

Among the rest of Missouri's residents of European ancestry, about one-fifth are Irish, and one-sixth claim English heritage. However, native-born Missourians trace their roots to many other nations, too.

African Americans

People of African descent first settled in Missouri in 1764 when Pierre Lacélde founded the trading post and village that would one day be the city of St. Louis. Both slaves and free men and women made their place in the new community. According to the 1799 census, the first accurate count taken, the city's population included 56 free Africans and African Americans, 268 slaves, and 601 people of European descent.

African-American Missourians have played a major role in shaping the history of their state from its earliest days. As slaves, settlers, farmers, and soldiers, African-Americans continued to leave their mark on the state throughout the 1800s. By the 1830s, they made up almost 18 percent of the state population, and their numbers were growing. Before 1866 it was illegal to educate African Americans in the state of Missouri. The Reverend John Berry Meachum found a way around the law by taking his students out on a boat in the middle of the Mississippi and holding class.

The slave Dred Scott was at the center of an infamous ruling by the US Supreme Court.

Dred Scott

Much of Missouri's history has been influenced by the fight over slavery that resulted in the Civil War. During the 1800s, some slaves tried to gain their freedom in US courts. In the 1850s, a former Missouri slave took his fight for freedom all the way to the US Supreme Court. Dred Scott had moved with his owner, Dr. John Emerson, in 1836 from St. Louis to Fort Snelling, in present-day Minnesota, where slavery was not allowed. Eventually, Dr. Emerson and Dred Scott moved back to St. Louis. This action prompted Scott to argue that he was no longer a slave since he had been taken to a territory where slavery was not allowed.

After pleading his case before state and federal circuit courts, the case went to the Supreme Court in Washington, DC. In a landmark judgment known as the Dred Scott

Maya Angelou

George Washington Carver

Sheryl Crow

1. Maya Angelou

Maya Angelou (1928–2014) was born Marguerite Johnson in St. Louis in 1928 but moved to Arkansas when her parents split up. With more than fifty honorary doctorate degrees, Dr. Angelou became a celebrated poet, memoirist, educator, dramatist, producer, actress, historian, filmmaker, and civil rights activist.

2. Yogi Berra

This baseball Hall of Famer from St. Louis is one of the best catchers ever. He played in fourteen World Series with the New York Yankees, and managed in two others. He is known for expressions, such as "It ain't over till it's over."

3. George Washington Carver

George Washington Carver was born into slavery in Diamond around 1864 (the exact date of his birth is unknown). Carver went on to become a famous scientist, inventor, and teacher. He invented hundreds of products using the peanut.

4. Sheryl Crow

Born in Kennett in 1962, Sheryl Crow graduated from the University of Missouri. After teaching music at an elementary school, she began singing in a local band. The Grammy-award winner has sold more than fifty million albums.

5. Walt Disney

Though born in Chicago, Walt Disney spent most of his childhood in Marceline and Kansas City, Missouri. In 1923, he founded the Walt Disney Company, one of the largest media companies in the world.

6. Jon Hamm

This St. Louis–born actor suffered the divorce of his parents and the death of his mother by the age of ten. He attended John Burroughs Preparatory School, and taught there before pursuing acting, landing his famous role as Don Draper in *Mad Men* in 2007.

7. Jesse James

Born in Kearney in 1847, Jesse and his brother Frank wandered throughout the United States robbing banks and trains. In 1882, members of his own gang shot and killed James in order to claim the reward for his capture.

8. Kate Spade

Born Katherine Noel Brosnahan in 1962 in Kansas City, Missouri, Kate Spade became famous for creating her trademark black nylon bags. After building an international accessories business, Spade branched out into new markets, such as fine china.

9. Mark Twain

Samuel Clemens, better known as Mark Twain, was born in Florida, Missouri, in 1835 and grew up in Hannibal. His novels *The Adventures of Tom Sawyer* and *The Adventures of Huckleberry Finn* are considered to be American classics.

10. Laura Ingalls Wilder

Born in Wisconsin, this author of beloved children's books lived in South Dakota, Minnesota, and Florida before settling permanently near Mansfield, Missouri, in July 1894. Wilder's classic stories are based on her own life on the frontier.

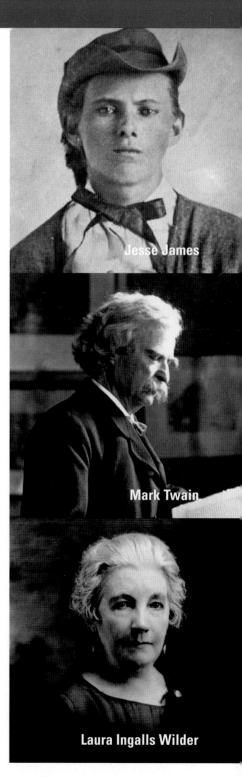

Jesse James

Mark Twain

Laura Ingalls Wilder

Who Missourians Are

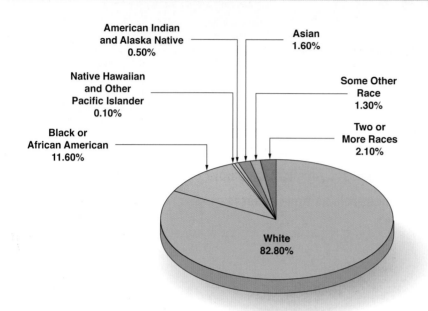

American Indian and Alaska Native 0.50%

Native Hawaiian and Other Pacific Islander 0.10%

Black or African American 11.60%

Asian 1.60%

Some Other Race 1.30%

Two or More Races 2.10%

White 82.80%

Total Population 5,988,927

Hispanic or Latino (of any race):
• 212,470 people (3.5%)

Note: The pie chart shows the racial breakdown of the state's population based on the categories used by the US Bureau of the Census. The Census Bureau reports information for Hispanics or Latinos separately, since they may be of any race. Percentages in the pie chart may not add to 100 because of rounding.

Source: US Bureau of the Census, 2010 Census

decision, the court ruled that African-Americans, whether slave or free, were not US citizens and did not have the right to pursue a case in court. It also ruled no one could have property taken from them without due process, even if that property was a person. Due process is fair treatment through the normal judicial system. The decision sparked a major controversy and only increased the bitterness and tension that existed between the North and the South.

After the Civil War ended in 1865, small African-American communities sprang up in what is known as the Little Dixie region of central Missouri. These towns grew out of a sense of newfound freedom and a desire for land, security, and independence. One of these towns was known as Little Africa. It was located on a rugged stretch of land southwest of the town of Roanoke, in Howard County. By the late 1870s, African-American settlers owned more than 300 acres (121 ha), almost doubling that amount by the end of the century. Eventually more and more houses were built in Little Africa. A church, a school, and neighborhoods appeared.

Mostly farmers, the town residents took advantage of the wealth that had come to the region from growing tobacco. By the early 1900s, though, tobacco production decreased, and the life of the town began to decline. Although by 1920 Little Africa was little more than a ghost town, it still stands as a bold new experiment in freedom, and a symbol of Missouri's strong, independent African-American community.

Today, African Americans make up about 12 percent of the state's population. Large communities are found in Missouri's cities—St. Louis in particular. Since arriving in Missouri, African Americans have made many important contributions to their state.

Unfortunately, recent events demonstrate that there is still work to be done to improve relations among the races in Missouri, as well as the United States in general. On August 9, 2014, an unarmed teenager named Michael Brown was shot and killed by a white police officer in Ferguson, a small city of about twenty-one thousand people in St. Louis County, not far from the city of St. Louis. The fatal shooting triggered nationwide protests and focused attention on other African-American deaths around the nation at the hands of police officers. This tragedy led to important discussions about how law enforcement treats minorities and what can be done to improve relations between the police and the communities they serve, no matter what race is involved.

Hispanic Americans

Hispanic communities are growing in Missouri. According to the 2000 census, the Hispanic-Latino population in Missouri was 118,617, but in 2010 the number increased to 212,470, an increase of 79 percent in just ten years. Hispanics now account for 3.5 percent of Missouri's population. That is not as large as some other states such as California, but the influence of Hispanic culture is important and growing.

Missouri's Hispanics work in many careers and own many businesses. According to the 2002 Economic Census, Hispanics owned more than 3,500 firms in the state.

One of Missouri's biggest challenges is to **assimilate** the growing Hispanic population into its English-speaking society. While speaking a different language can make it difficult for some Hispanics to communicate, it can also provide an opportunity for current Missouri businesses. Companies that can talk to Hispanics in their native tongue can expand their business into new markets.

Asian Americans

The Asian and Pacific Island population has increased in Missouri from 0.8 percent of the total population in 1990 to 1.2 percent in 2000 and 1.6 percent in 2010. Although all Missouri counties have some Asian residents, most live in cities. St. Louis County is home to Missouri's largest Asian population, and Jackson County (Kansas City) ranked second. Not only do those two counties have the largest Asian population, but they also experienced the state's greatest Asian population growth.

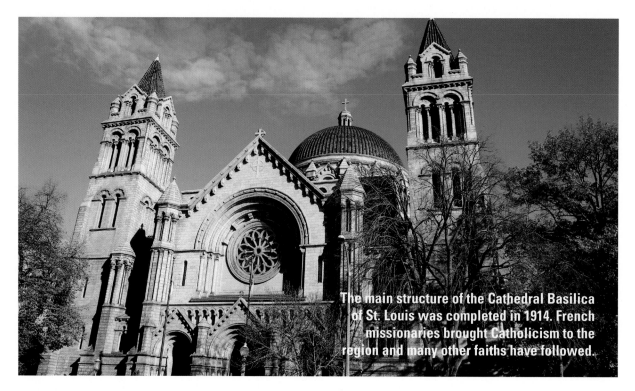

The main structure of the Cathedral Basilica of St. Louis was completed in 1914. French missionaries brought Catholicism to the region and many other faiths have followed.

Immigrants

Missouri is also adding large populations of new immigrants who bring even more diversity to the Show-Me State. Immigrants who were born in foreign countries make up almost 4 percent of the state's population. Most settle in Missouri's larger urban centers or in the southwestern part of the state, where jobs are easier to find. Immigrants are not only important to the state's economy as workers, they supply billions of dollars in tax revenue and purchasing power. They also add their own culture and traditions to the colorful tapestry that is life in Missouri today.

Slower Population Growth

Over the last one hundred years, Missouri has fallen from the seventh most populous state in the nation to eighteenth. In 1910, Missouri's population of 3.29 million residents was smaller than only six other states: New York, Pennsylvania, Illinois, Ohio, Texas, and Massachusetts. By 2010 it had dropped behind an additional twelve. Although Missouri has grown in population each decade since statehood, it has not done so at a rate to keep pace with the rest of the nation. Overall, Missouri's population increased 81.2 percent from 1910 (3.29 million) to 2010 (5.98 million), compared to a 234.8 percent increase for the United States generally. Unlike sunbelt states where net immigration is the primary cause of population increase, Missouri's increases are mainly due to natural increase (births minus deaths). This pattern is typical for the states in the Midwest.

Many Faiths

Beginning in the late seventeenth century, French missionaries brought Roman Catholicism to what is now Missouri. Immigration from Germany, Ireland, Italy, and Eastern Europe swelled the Catholic population during the nineteenth century, and Roman Catholicism remains the largest single Christian denomination today, though the Evangelical Protestants taken as a whole outnumber Catholics. Baptist preachers crossed the Mississippi River into Missouri in the late 1790s, and the state's first Methodist church was organized about 1806. Immigrants from Germany included not only Roman Catholics, but also many Lutherans.

The Mormons

In the 1830s, Mormonism commanded center stage in Missouri politics. Joseph Smith and the church he founded in New York State in 1830 quickly gained converts, attracting considerable attention throughout the northeastern United States. That same year, Smith sent a handful of missionaries to Missouri's western border to preach the "restored gospel" to the Native American tribes concentrated there. In 1831, Smith proclaimed that God had designated western Missouri as the place where "Zion" would be "gathered" in anticipation of Christ's second coming. His small band of missionaries soon became a steady stream of converts anxious to establish Zion in Missouri.

However, other Missouri residents felt threatened by the Mormons. Violence broke out in the 1830s and continued to get worse. On October 30, 1838, an organized mob launched a surprise attack on the small Mormon community of Haun's Mill, killing eighteen unsuspecting men and boys. Over the next year, around eight thousand Mormon Church members, often ragged and deprived of their property, left Missouri for Illinois.

Education

Education in Missouri is provided by public and private schools, colleges, and universities, and a variety of public library systems. The largest university in the state is the University of Missouri in Columbia. Other universities include the University of Missouri–St. Louis, University of Missouri–Kansas City, the Missouri University of Science and Technology, and Missouri State University in Springfield.

Arts and Culture

Examples of Missouri arts and culture can be found everywhere in the Show-Me State. World-class art institutions and museums, Civil War battlefields, and historical sites fill the state. The city of Branson is especially well known as a center for live music performances.

★ 10 ★ KEY EVENTS ★

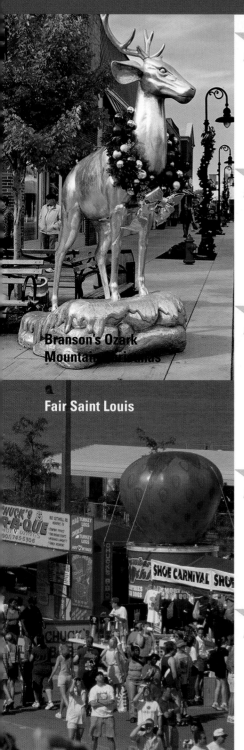

Branson's Ozark Mountain Christmas

Fair Saint Louis

1. Branson's Ozark Mountain Christmas

This annual celebration begins in November and lasts through New Year's Eve. Branson undergoes a wintry change as the city lights up with the Festival of Lights. There are music performances, parades, Christmas tree lightings, and fireworks.

2. Fair Saint Louis

The Gateway City hosts this three-day event known as one of the best Fourth of July celebrations in the country. Top musical acts, educational activities, and air shows all serve as a warm-up to a spectacular fireworks display.

3. Great Pershing Balloon Derby

This hot air balloon festival happens each September near Brookfield, Missouri. The three-day festival draws balloonists from all over the country. It is recognized by the Balloon Federation of America (BFA) as the longest running event in the nation.

4. Heart of America Shakespeare Festival

Held each June and July in Kansas City's Southmoreland Park, this is one of America's largest free Shakespeare festivals. In addition to attending the Bard's plays, audience members can also attend skits, comedy acts, and lectures.

5. Heritage Festival & Craft Show

This Columbia event celebrates Missouri's proud heritage each September. As traditional tradesmen demonstrate their "lost arts," kids can also listen to ghost stories and learn how to milk a cow, braid a rope, and make a candle!

MISSOURI ★ ★ ★ ★

6. Missouri State Fair

Since the first Fair in 1901, thousands of Missouri families have made the annual "pilgrimage" to Sedalia. In addition to music, food, and other entertainment choices, the fair features competitions in livestock and crop production for ribbons, recognition, and cash.

7. Neosho Fall Festival Autumn Harvest

This fair is held in the city of Neosho each October. Festivalgoers are treated to traditional arts and crafts demonstrations, "coaster car" races (think soap box derby), food booths, inflatable obstacle courses, and musical performances.

8. Ozark Mountain Festival

The Ozark Mountain Festival in Eminence is a celebration of the Ozarks culture and heritage, and recreational activities. The event is an all-day affair on the Old Jacks Fork Bridge Walkway, with demonstrations, food booths, charity auctions, and more.

9. Pony Express PumpkinFest

This fun-filled event, held every fall in St. Joseph, features rides, games, and a parade. They all lead up to the main event, the lighting of a wall of more than 750 jack-o'-lanterns called the Great Pumpkin Mountain.

10. "Trick or Treat" Through Missouri History

This family-friendly event in Columbia is presented by the State Historical Society of Missouri. Kids and their parents are invited to come in costume to learn about crafts, bats, pumpkins, and the ghosts of Missouri's past.

Pony Express PumpkinFest

"Trick or Treat" Through Missouri History

A statue of Thomas Jefferson, the third President of the United States, stands outside the state capitol in Jefferson City, which was named for him.

How the Government Works

Missouri's state constitution was adopted in 1945. The state had three earlier versions. They were approved in 1820, 1865, and 1875. This series of constitutions shows that the state is flexible and able to change with the times.

Each year brings new challenges and issues that the lawmakers and citizens of Missouri must face and solve. In order to do that, Missourians work together. They know that in order to improve life for all the state's residents, they must be open to new ideas and opinions. In Missouri politics, compromise is key.

Local Leaders

Missourians serve in their state government at all levels. Voters in each of the state's 114 counties choose local leaders to be in charge of the day-to-day business of running Missouri's cities and towns. To be sure things run smoothly, a variety of officials are needed. Voters typically elect county commissioners, treasurers, tax collectors, coroners, sheriffs, and attorneys, just to name a few. Missouri's larger urban centers also select mayors and city councils to address their city's affairs.

The third version of the state capitol building was completed in 1917. It houses murals by artist Thomas Hart Benton, a Neosho native from a family of politicians.

Branches of State Government

Missouri's state government consists of the legislative branch, which passes laws; the executive branch, which carries out the laws; and the judicial branch, which interprets the laws and administers justice.

Little Big City

Missouri's state capital, Jefferson City, is an unusually small size for a state capital. Only forty-three thousand people live there, and it is ranked fifteenth in population in the state.

Executive

The governor is the head of the executive branch. He or she is elected to a four-year term and can only serve for two terms. Aiding the governor are important officials who help run the state. They include the lieutenant governor, the secretary of state, the state treasurer, and the attorney general.

In addition to signing bills into law, Missouri's governor has many other important responsibilities. The governor appoints people to serve on many of the state's boards and commissions. He or she can also appoint someone to fill a vacancy in one of the state's US Senate seats if a Senator is unable to finish a term of office. The governor also commands the state's National Guard, prepares a budget for the state, and grants pardons.

Harry S. Truman is the only Missouri native to lead the United States.

The lieutenant governor's job is to take over the job of governor if the governor is unable to finish his or her term. The lieutenant governor also leads the state senate and casts a vote in case of a tie.

Legislative

The state legislature is known as the General Assembly. It has two chambers, or parts. The state senate has 34 members, while the state house of representatives has 163. Senators serve for four years while Representatives serve for two. They help to create the laws that are needed to make Missouri run smoothly.

Judicial

The state's highest court, the Supreme Court, is made up of seven justices, or judges. The state Court of Appeals is divided into three districts. In addition, the state has circuit courts, associate circuit courts, and municipal courts. These lower courts handle a wide range of cases.

United States Senate and Congress

Like all other states, Missouri voters cast their ballots for President and Vice President of the United States. They also choose people to represent them in the US Congress in Washington, DC. Missouri voters elect two US Senators and eight members of the US House of Representatives.

From Bill to Law

Ideas for laws often come directly from the people. Citizens can contact their elected officials and share their ideas on how to improve life in their state. Bills may be introduced to the legislature by either senators or representatives in the state assembly.

When the bill is proposed, it is assigned a number, and its title is read to the lawmakers. The bill is then sent to a committee. A committee is a small group of legislators who look into the bill more closely. They also hold a public hearing. That way, the people of Missouri have the chance to express their opinions and tell the lawmakers how they feel about the potential new law. After all, laws affect the lives of everyone in the state. Missouri's legislators want to be sure everyone has had their say.

When the public hearing is over, the committee meets to vote. If they are in favor of the bill, they send it back to either the Senate or the House of Representatives—whichever chamber of the assembly first proposed it. If the committee changes certain parts of the bill, then the house or the senate must consider and debate those changes as well. The bill is then placed on what is called the "perfection calendar." When its turn comes in the order of business, the bill is debated. Lawmakers consider its good points and those areas that still need to be improved. When the bill and all its amendments, or changes, have been accepted, a vote is then taken to declare the bill perfected. That means that a majority of the legislators are happy with the bill.

After the bill is perfected, it is then read and voted on again. This extra step gives Missouri's lawmakers another chance to be sure the bill is a good measure for the state to adopt. If the bill passes this additional vote, it is then sent to the other chamber of Missouri's legislature for their discussion and approval. There it begins the same process all over again.

The lawmakers in the other half of the legislature form their own committee, hold a hearing, and then hold a series of votes. If they request changes to the bill, both chambers of the legislature must approve those changes. When the bill reaches its final form and both sides of the legislature are happy with its terms, it is declared "truly agreed to and finally passed." The state speaker of the house and the president of the state senate then sign the bill.

Next, the bill goes to the governor. If the governor signs it, the bill officially becomes a law. However, if the governor vetoes, or rejects, the bill, it then goes back to the legislature. Two-thirds of the members of each house must still be in favor of the bill to overturn the governor's veto and to make it into a law.

Missouri Voters

More than four million people are registered to vote in Missouri. Missouri does not require party registration, so it is difficult to tell how many voters describe themselves as Democratic, Republican, or Independent. However, the results of recent elections indicate

Residents in Ferguson and across the state used their right to protest after a young African-American man was shot and killed by police in 2014.

that Republicans are the stronger party by far, and elections in some districts show Republicans running unopposed by Democrats.

As of 2015, Missouri's governor is a Democrat but Republicans control the legislature. In the 2014 statewide elections, Republicans strengthened their grip on the Missouri General Assembly, holding 118 of 163 seats in the house of representatives (72.4 percent) and 25 of 34 seats (73.5 percent) in the senate. That meant that Republicans held what is called a veto-proof super majority in both houses. Since Republicans control more than two-thirds of the votes in both houses, they can vote to override the governor and pass a bill into law even if the governor does not approve it.

Getting Involved

In communities across Missouri, students have become actively involved in shaping their state. They have even proposed measures that were eventually approved by the legislature. Most of these measures have involved the adoption of official state symbols. Schoolchildren in Lee's Summit were responsible for getting the crinoid adopted as the state fossil. Marshfield's schoolchildren had the paddlefish named the state's aquatic animal, while students in Glasgow worked to get the channel catfish approved as the state's official fish. The Eastern black walnut became the state tree nut when, in 1990, Stockton's fourth graders drafted the bill.

POLITICAL FIGURES
FROM MISSOURI

Dick Gephardt:
US Representative, 1977-2005

The St. Louis-born Dick Gephardt received a law degree from the University of Michigan before serving fourteen terms in Congress. He was the House majority leader from 1989 to 1995 and the minority leader until 2003. He twice ran for the presidential nomination of the Democratic Party, the second time in 2004.

Claire McCaskill:
US Senator, 2007-

Born in Rolla and raised in Columbus, Claire McCaskill is the first woman from Missouri elected to the US Senate. She served as the state auditor for Missouri for eight years before going to Washington. McCaskill has spoken out against sexual violence, and in 2015 criticized the television show *Game of Thrones* for a sexually violent scene.

Harry S. Truman:
US President, 1945-1953

Harry S. Truman was born in Lamar, Missouri, on May 8, 1884 and also lived in Grandview, Independence, and Kansas City, Missouri. After serving as a US Senator and Vice President, he became President in 1945 when president Franklin D. Roosevelt died. He made the decision to drop the atomic bomb on Japan in 1945.

MISSOURI
YOU CAN MAKE A DIFFERENCE

Contacting Lawmakers

To find contact information for Missouri legislators, go to this website:

www.moga.mo.gov

There you will find links to the contact information for state senators and representatives.

To find your United States Senators and Representatives, go to this website:

www.contactingthecongress.org

Enter your address in the box at the left, and hit submit. You will be given links to your congressional representatives.

Driving a Change

Rick Worth owns a motorcycle dealership in Kansas City, Missouri. He wasn't allowed to sell motorcycles on Sunday because a state law, called a "**blue law**," banned certain activities on Sundays, including selling motorcycles. Worth believed the law cost him business. His biggest competitor was located just over the state line in Kansas, where Sunday motorcycle sales were permitted.

Worth decided to try and get the Missouri law changed. He began meeting with state officials in 2013. "The senators and representatives from the house I've spoken to, nearly half didn't realize there was a law to prevent me from selling on Sunday," said Worth.

Getting rid of the law was difficult. One problem was that the law also banned the sale of automobiles on Sunday, and Missouri car dealers did not want that changed. The state general assembly finally introduced a bill to change the law (without including automobiles) on February 5, 2014. Worth traveled to the state capital, Jefferson City, to testify in favor of the bill. After being passed in the state house of representatives, the bill moved to the state senate. Both chambers passed a revised bill on May 13, and the Governor Jay Nixon signed it on June 23.

Branson is a major tourist destination, and the entertainment center on 76 Country Boulevard attracts people from around the country.

Making a Living

Missouri's location has helped create a strong state economy. The state lies in the middle of the nation, making it convenient to ship and receive goods from the north, east, south and west by air, rail, and truck. Missouri's rivers provide easy access to shipping and ports around the country.

Ever since French trappers first braved the untamed wilds of east-central Missouri, St. Louis has been an important center for transportation and trade. In the years since, banking and manufacturing have also blossomed in the area. On the other side of the state, Kansas City built its wealth on agriculture. Cattle and grain have been processed and sold there since the 1800s.

The state's industries are not concentrated only within its major urban centers, though. To the southwest, cities such as Springfield are among the state's fastest growing. Many businesses have been drawn to the area through the years. Now the region sports a thriving trade in telecommunications, transportation, and warehouse-related businesses. In the other corner of the state, in southeastern Missouri, Cape Girardeau is ideally located. Its position along the Mississippi River makes it another important center for shipping and commerce.

No matter where Missouri's citizens are employed, they work hard to make sure their state will continue to succeed.

Farming

Missouri is still farm country. Farms cover about two-thirds of the state's total area. Missouri's farms are almost equally devoted to livestock and crop production, with livestock holding a slight advantage. About 53 percent of the state's farm revenue comes from livestock and 47 percent comes from vegetables, grains, and fruits.

About fifty-nine thousand farms raise livestock, one of Missouri's biggest products. Missouri ranks as one of the nation's leading producers of beef cattle, pigs, and turkeys. Most of the cattle and hog farms are located north of the Missouri River as well as in the western and southwestern portions of the state. Dairy farms are grouped there as well. On the other hand, most of the state's turkey farms are located in central Missouri.

Missouri farms also produce many different crops. Soybeans and corn are the state's two biggest, but many others are grown as well. Sorghum, hay, wheat, cotton, peaches, apples, and grapes are also key Show-Me State crops.

Missouri ranks seventh among all states in soybean production. Crushing facilities take whole soybeans and process them to make soy oil and soybean meal. Most of the soybean meal is used as animal feed, but some is used for human foods. The soy oil has many food and industrial uses. Soybean farms are found mostly on the Northern Plains, north of the Missouri River.

Much of the corn grown in Missouri is used to feed the state's livestock. It is also used to make ethanol, a type of fuel mainly mixed with gasoline for use in automobiles. Corn thrives across the state, but most farms are located in central Missouri, while the sorghum district is more to the east.

The presence of lead brought many miners to Missouri.

Mining

In the early days of the territory, mining helped to make Missouri strong. Galena, a type of lead ore, was first unearthed near Potosi in 1701. Since the 1720s, with the discovery of major deposits at Mine La Motte, near Fredericktown, galena's importance has only grown. Mines sprang up throughout the southeastern portion of the state, which became unofficially known as the lead district. From 1870 to 1965, almost all of the state's lead came from there. At the same time, large amounts of zinc were produced from this area as well. Zinc, along with copper and silver, is collected when the iron ore is processed.

Today, Missouri continues to be a mining leader. Since the 1960s, though, the industry has found newer and richer deposits of galena in an area now called the Viburnum Trend, located to the west of the old lead district. Today, the state accounts for about 90 percent of the nation's total lead production.

Missouri also ranks high in the production of **fireclay**, lime, cement, and crushed stone. The cement and stone usually come from Missouri's limestone quarries found along the Mississippi River. Oil, gas, and coal are produced in smaller amounts, but are still vital to the state's economy.

Iron mining is a fairly new development in Missouri. The Pea Ridge Mine, near Sullivan, was developed in the 1950s. Though companies operating the mine have faced financial difficulties, new investors recently reopened the mine and, in May 2011, opened a new magnetite processing plant as well. Magnetite is a form of magnetic iron ore that is used to make iron, steel, and other alloys. An alloy is a metal made from two or more metallic elements.

Sparks fly as a welder works in a Kansas City factory. Missouri manufactures a lot of large-scale transportation equipment.

Manufacturing

Over the past few decades, thousands of manufacturers have opened or expanded their businesses in the Show-Me State. These new and larger ventures have joined the several major companies already located in the state. Many of these giants are considered leaders in their field.

Some Missouri companies specialize in technology related to research on genes, the information that is stored inside cells. Each of these industries requires smart, well-trained workers, and business leaders know those workers can be found in Missouri.

★ 10 KEY★INDUSTRIES

Argiculture

Automotive

1. Aerospace

Missouri's growing aerospace manufacturing sector includes companies that make aircraft, aircraft engines, guided missile systems, and space vehicles. Aerospace products and parts represent 13.5 percent of the sector's employment.

2. Agriculture

In 2011, the corn industry contributed 65,960 jobs and $4.3 billion to the state's economy. Soybean sales often exceed $1 billion a year.

3. Automotive

Missouri has continuously distinguished itself as a Top Ten state for automotive vehicle production. Ford and General Motors both recently announced major expansions in Missouri, and electric car makers have also located in the state.

4. Bioscience

Missouri claims some of the most prestigious hospitals, medical schools, and bioscience companies in the country. Missouri is home to companies such as Pfizer, a pharmaceutical manufacturer; Monsanto, an agricultural chemical manufacturer; and Bausch & Lomb Surgical, a medical equipment manufacturer.

5. Brewing

The North American headquarters of Anheuser-Busch InBev, the world's largest maker of beer, is in St. Louis. Caves under the city provided natural refrigeration when the company started in 1860. The Busch family first used refrigerated railroad cars to keep their products fresh for longer shipping.

6. Cattle

As of January 2015, Missouri ranked sixth among all US states as a producer of beef cattle. The livestock industry is centered in the southwestern portion of the state. Cattle provide much of the income for the state's livestock farmers.

7. Food Manufacturing

In 2013, food producers ranked as Missouri's top manufacturing employer for a fourth consecutive year. Missouri's central location and its strength in agriculture help make the state a good place for food companies to manufacture and ship their products.

8. Lead

Approximately 90 percent of lead produced in the United States comes from Missouri, making it the nation's top producer. Lead is the state's most valuable mineral. It is mostly found in southeastern Missouri in Iron, Reynolds, and Washington Counties.

9. Pet Food and Animal Health

Missouri companies now represent 56 percent of worldwide animal health, diagnostics, and pet food sales. The area around Manhattan, Kansas, and Columbia, Missouri, is home to more than three hundred animal health companies, the largest concentration in the world.

10. Tourism

Missouri's tourism industry provides more than 280,000 jobs and generates nearly $11 billion in income to the state's economy each year.

Cattle

Pet Food and Animal Health

Recipe for Black Walnut Cake

Missouri is the world's top producer of black walnuts. The following recipe uses black walnuts to make a delicious cake:

What You Need

For the Cake

1 cup (236.5 milliliters) butter

½ cup (118.2 mL) vegetable shortening

1 cup (236.5 mL) sugar

2 cups (473 mL) firmly packed brown sugar

5 eggs

3 cups (709 mL) all-purpose flour

½ tsp. (2.46 mL) baking powder

¼ tsp. (1.23 mL) salt

1 tbsp. (14.8 mL) vanilla extract

1 cup (118.2 mL) finely chopped black walnuts

For the Icing

¼ cup (59 mL) butter, softened

1 pkg. (3 oz or 88.7 mL) cream cheese, softened

1 lb. (0.45 kg) powdered sugar

2–3 tbsp. (29.6–44.4 mL) milk

What To Do

- Preheat the oven to 325°F (163°C).
- Using an electric mixer, cream butter and shortening together.
- Gradually add white and brown sugar, beating at medium speed. Add eggs one at a time, beating well after each addition.
- Sift flour, baking powder, and salt together and add to creamed mix.
- Stir in vanilla and walnuts.
- Pour into greased and floured 10-inch tube pan. Bake for one hour or until a wooden toothpick inserted near the center comes out clean. Cool in pan for fifteen minutes, then remove and cool on wire rack.
- Prepare frosting by creaming butter and cream cheese together. Add powdered sugar and milk, beating until it reaches spreading consistency.

Ready to Mix

The first ready-mix food to be sold commercially was Aunt Jemima pancake flour. It was invented in St. Joseph, Missouri, and introduced in 1899.

Other Missouri cities and towns host their own major business ventures. Kansas City is home to the headquarters of Hallmark Cards. The next time you send or receive a birthday card, there is a good chance it was created in western Missouri. Because Kansas City lies at the heart of the Winter Wheat Belt, there are several large flour mills in the area as well.

Major automakers also have plants sprinkled across the state. Ford, General Motors, and Chrysler have helped to make Missouri a leading producer of transportation equipment. Each day workers produce barges, railroad cars, truck trailers, and the bodies of automobiles. Chemicals are also big business in the state. Missouri factories pump out paint, health products, soap, and insect sprays for farms and gardens.

Retail and Services

A large amount of Missouri's earnings come from its service workers. These hard workers include doctors, nurses, hotel and office workers, and many others. Adding to the state's earning power are bankers, real-estate agents, teachers, railroad and barge workers, and

Telephone operators work at a busy call center. Employers are drawn to the state because of its talented and educated workforce.

Johnson's Shut-Ins State Park draws people from near and far to its hiking, swimming, and camping facilities.

Day Trip

Situated within a day's drive of 50 percent of the US population, Branson and the Tri-Lakes area serve up to sixty-five thousand visitors daily.

telephone company employees, to name just a few of the countless ways Missourians earn a living.

Retail sales are also important to Missouri's economy. With such a heavily agricultural state, it is not surprising that the sale of machines and farm-related equipment is important to Missouri's economy. Other leading retail areas include restaurants, shopping malls, and car dealers.

In recent years, tourism has played a larger role in building the state's wealth. The state's economy is helped by the money people spend while staying at hotels, shopping in stores, and dining in Missouri's eateries. Branson, a resort town outside of Springfield, draws top performers, some of whom have built permanent theaters in the town. Tour buses roll through the area, filled with eager visitors.

Big cities such as St. Louis offer many attractions for tourists. These include the Gateway Arch, Union Station, Forest Park, the St. Louis Zoo, and many museums. Kansas City offers visitors more miles of boulevards than Paris and more fountains than any city except for Rome.

Missouri is home to several professional athletic teams. St. Louis hosts the Cardinals (baseball), the Rams (football), and the Blues (hockey), while Kansas City boasts the Royals (baseball), and the Chiefs (football). Money spent on game tickets and souvenirs helps the state economy.

People also come to the state to enjoy Missouri's natural wonders. Throughout the year, visitors fish, hike, and explore the different parts of the state. The Ozarks in particular have been a top destination for visitors from around the United States and the world.

Renewable Energy

Although Missouri's renewable energy industry is less developed than some of its neighboring states, it has strong potential for growth, being especially well suited for wind and **bioenergy** production. The state's large tracts of windy land and fertile soil, located relatively close to dense, energy-consuming urban centers, put Missouri in a prime position to become a national leader in renewable energy.

Studies show that a strong, local renewable energy industry in Missouri would create tens of thousands of jobs and provide substantial new sources of income for farmers. By developing wind power, making biomass energy from agricultural waste, and growing dedicated energy crops to make advanced biofuels, Missouri can keep its energy dollars at home and even start exporting energy to other states.

Missouri has already established a Renewable Energy Standard that will require 15 percent of the state's energy to come from renewable sources by 2021. The state has adopted policies and tax policies to help support the renewable energy industry's advancement.

The state's residents know there is much that makes Missouri special. They look to their state with a sense of pride, and they stand committed to making it the best it can be.

MISSOURI
STATE MAP

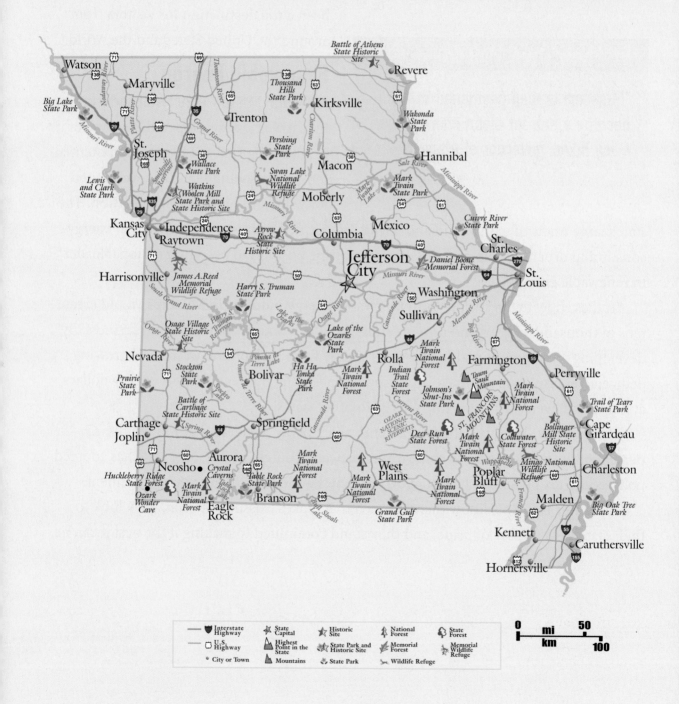

Watson
Maryville
Big Lake State Park
St. Joseph
Lewis and Clark State Park
Kansas City
Harrisonville
Nevada
Prairie State Park
Carthage
Joplin
Neosho
Huckleberry Ridge State Forest
Ozark Wonder Cave
Aurora
Crystal Caverns
Branson
Eagle Rock

Trenton
Wallace State Park
Watkins Woolen Mill State Park and State Historic Site
Independence
Raytown
Arrow Rock State Historic Site
James A. Reed Memorial Wildlife Refuge
Harry S. Truman State Park
Osage Village State Historic Site
Stockton State Park
Bolivar
Battle of Carthage State Historic Site
Springfield
Mark Twain National Forest
Table Rock State Park

Thousand Hills State Park
Kirksville
Pershing State Park
Swan Lake National Wildlife Refuge
Macon
Moberly
Columbia
Jefferson City
Lake of the Ozarks
Ha Ha Tonka State Park
Mark Twain National Forest
Rolla
Indian Trail State Forest
West Plains
Mark Twain National Forest
Grand Gulf State Park

Battle of Athens State Historic Site
Revere
Wakonda State Park
Hannibal
Mark Twain State Park
Mexico
Cuivre River State Park
St. Charles
Daniel Boone Memorial Forest
Washington
Sullivan
St. Louis
Mark Twain National Forest
Farmington
Taum Sauk Mountain
Johnson's Shut-Ins State Park
St. Francois Mountains
Mark Twain National Forest
Perryville
Trail of Tears State Park
Cape Girardeau
Bollinger Mill State Historic Site
Collwater State Forest
Charleston
Deer Run State Forest
Mark Twain National Forest
Poplar Bluff
Mingo National Wildlife Refuge
Malden
Big Oak Tree State Park
Kennett
Caruthersville
Hornersville

Ozark National Scenic Riverways

Legend
- Interstate Highway
- U.S. Highway
- City or Town
- State Capital
- Highest Point in the State
- Mountains
- Historic Site
- State Park and Historic Site
- State Park
- National Forest
- Memorial Forest
- Wildlife Refuge
- State Forest
- Memorial Wildlife Refuge

0   mi   50
0   km   100

MISSOURI ★ ★ ★
MAP SKILLS

1. What interstate highway connects St. Louis with Kansas City?

2. What is the nearest city to Trail of Tears State Park?

3. What cave is located in the southwest corner of Missouri?

4. What is the State Capital of Missouri?

5. What Missouri city lies furthest to the west?

6. What is the highest point in Missouri?

7. What two rivers meet at St. Louis?

8. The Lake of the Ozarks is located in what part of Missouri? North, South, East, West or Central?

9. The state park located just northwest of the Lake of the Ozarks is named after a US President. What is the President's name?

10. One Missouri city has the same name as a US State. Another city has the same name as a foreign country. Can you name the two cities?

Truman Reservoir

Taum Sauk Mountain

10. Nevada and Mexico
9. Harry S. Truman
8. Central
7. The Mississippi and Missouri Rivers
6. Taum Sauk Mountain
5. Watson
4. Jefferson City
3. Ozark Wonder Cave
2. Cape Girardeau
1. Interstate 70 (I-70)

State Flag, Seal, and Song

Missouri's state flag consists of three horizontal stripes of red, white, and blue, representing valor, purity, and justice. The center white stripe shows the Missouri coat-of-arms, circled by a blue band containing twenty-four stars, Missouri being the twenty-fourth state.

The center of the state seal depicts two grizzly bears, which represent the strength and bravery of the state's residents. The bears are holding a shield that contains the United States coat-of-arms, another grizzly bear, and a silver crescent moon. The crescent symbolizes the idea that Missouri would grow like the crescent moon. Around the edges of the shield are the words "United We Stand Divided We Fall." Missouri's state motto, "The welfare of the people shall be supreme law," appears in Latin below the shield but above the Roman numerals for 1820, the year Missouri began its functions as a state.

The helmet above the shield represents state sovereignty, and the large star atop the helmet surrounded by twenty-three smaller stars signified Missouri's status as the twenty-fourth state.

"The Missouri Waltz" became the state song on June 30, 1949. It had gained popularity after President Harry S. Truman played the song on the piano at the White House. The words are by James Royce Shannon, but the origin of the music is in dispute. Some credit it to orchestra leader John Valentine Eppel. To view the lyrics, visit: **www.sos.mo.gov/archives/history/song.asp**

Glossary

aquifer   A layer of rock or sand that can absorb, hold, and transmit groundwater.

assimilate   To adapt or adjust to the customs of a group of people or a nation.

bioenergy   A type of energy produced from plant and animal materials that can be grown again.

blue laws   Laws that do not allow certain businesses to open on Sunday or to sell certain items on that day.

convention   A large meeting of people who come to a place, usually for several days, to talk about their shared work or interests or to make decisions as a group.

fireclay   Clay capable of withstanding high temperatures.

funnel   A device shaped like a hollow cone with a tube extending from the point. Tornadoes start as a rapidly rotating funnel-shaped cloud extending downward. If it touches the ground it is called a tornado.

immigrant   A person who comes to a country from a foreign country to live permanently.

migrate   To move from one country or place to live or work in another.

reservations [Native American]   An area of land in the US that is kept separate as a place for Native Americans to live.

reservoir   A place (like a lake, usually man-made) that is used to store a large supply of water for people to use for their needs.

slave   Someone who is legally owned by another person and is forced to work for that person without pay.

tornado   A violent, destructive, rapidly moving storm in which powerful winds move around a central point.

tram   A four-wheeled, open, box-shaped wagon or iron car that runs on tracks.

More About Missouri

BOOKS

Cromwell, Sharon. *Dred Scott v. Sandford: A Slave's Case for Freedom and Citizenship.* North Mankato, MN: Compass Point Books, 2009.

Lago, Mary Ellen. *Missouri.* Danbury, CT: Children's Press, 2009.

Lanier, Wendy. *What Was the Missouri Compromise?: And Other Questions About the Struggle over Slavery.* Minneapolis, MN: Lerner Publishing Group, 2012.

Marsico, Katie. *The Missouri River.* North Mankato, MN: Cherry Lake Publishing, 2013.

WEBSITES

Office of Missouri Governor

governor.mo.gov

Official Missouri State Website

www.mo.gov

Official Missouri Tourism Website

www.visitmo.com/

ABOUT THE AUTHORS

Doug Sanders is a writer living in New York City. He attended graduate school in St. Louis, where he loved attending Blues games and eating Ted Drewe's frozen custard.

Gerry Boehme was born in New York City, graduated from The Newhouse School at Syracuse University and now lives on Long Island with his wife and two children. He is an author, editor, and a businessperson and has spoken at international conferences.

Index

Page numbers in **boldface** are illustrations. Entries in **boldface** are glossary terms.

African Americans, 15, 46–47, 50–51, **61**
agriculture, 23, 65, 68–69, **68**
aquifer, 13
assimilate, 51

Bagnell Dam, 13, **16**, 43
bioenergy, 73
blue laws, 63
Boone, Daniel, 29, **29**
Bootheel, 16–17
Branson, 13, 15, 53–54, **64**, 65, 72

Cape Girardeau, 25, 65
capital, *see* Jefferson City
caves and caverns, 13–14, **13**, **14**, 68
Channel catfish, 20, **20**, 61
cities, *see* Branson, Independence, Kansas City, Springfield, St. Louis
Civil War, 15, 36–38, **38**, 47, 50, 53

climate, 17–19
convention, 37–38

explorers, 24–25, 28, 43

factories, 39–40, 42, 71
farms and farming, **6**, 8–9, 17, 23–24, 26, 29, 31, 37, 40–42, 50, 66, 69, 72–73
fireclay, 67
fish and fishing, 19–20, **20**, 61
forests, 7–9, 17–19, 24
fossils, 4, 61
fruits, 21, 66
funnel, 18

Gateway Arch, 14, 72
glaciers, 8–9

immigrant, 40, 46, 52–53
Independence, 14, 34, 36, 42, 62

Jackson, Claiborne F., 37–38
Jefferson City, 56, 58, 63
Jefferson, Thomas, 36, **56**
Jolliet, Louis, 25, 28, 43

Kansas (state), 36–37, 43, 63
Kansas City, 15, 31, 34, **34**, 35, 38–39, 48–49, 51, 53–54, 62–63, 65, 71–73

Laclède, Pierre, 28, 47
Lake of the Ozarks, 13, 16, **16**, 43
livestock, 31, 55, 66, 69
Louisiana Purchase, 29, **31**, 43

manufacturing, 65, 67–69
Marquette, Jacques, 25, 28, 43
Marvel Cave, 13, **13**
migrate, 25–26
mills, 31, 39, 71
minerals, 4, 8, 16, 29, 69
mines and mining, 9, 14, 28–29, 40, 66–67,
missionaries, 28, 52–53
Mississippi River, 7, 9, 12, 15, 24–26, 28, 53, 65, 67
Missouri Compromise, 33, 36–37, 43
Missouri River, 5, 7–9, **8**, 24–26, **25**, 34, 46, 66

Index

mountains,
St. Francois, 9, 12
Taum Sauk, 12, **12**, **75**
Native Americans, 15,
23–28, 31–32, 35, 43,
45–46, **46**, 53
Delaware, 25–26
Osage, 24–27, **24**, 32, 35, 43
Otoe, 24, 26

Northern Plains, 7, 8–9, 66

Osage River, 13, 24, 43
Ozark Mountains, 31, 34,
54–55

Ozark Plateau, 9, 12–13, 19,
34

reservations, 27, 32, 43
reservoir, 13, 75

Santa Fe Trail, 34, 36, 39
Scott, Dred, 47, **47**, 50
settlers, 7, 17, 28–29, 31–32,
36, 45–47, 50
slave, 32–33, 36–38, 43,
46–48, 50
soybeans, 8, 17, 66
Springfield, 14, 19, 34, 37,
53, 65, 72

St. Louis, 7, 14, 28, **33**,
34–35, **34**, 39, 42, 45,
47–49, 51, 53, 62, 65, 68,
72–73

tornado, 18, 43
tourism, 69, 72
tram, 14
Truman, Harry S., 14, 42,
59, 62, **62**
Twain, Mark, 15, 49, **49**

War of 1812, 31
World Wars I and II, 40–41